Ludlow

Ludlow

A Verse-Novel

DAVID MASON

RED HEN PRESS | *Los Angeles, California*

Book design by Mark E. Cull

Cover art by David Ligare. "Pastorale Landscape", 2000, oil on canvas, 40" x 56",
courtesy of the artist and Koplin Del Rio Gallery, os Angeles, CA.

ISBN 10: 1-59709-083-2 (tradepaper)
ISBN 13: 978-1-59709-083-4 (tradepaper)
ISBN 10: 1-59709-084-0 (clothbound)
ISBN 13: 978-1-59709-084-1 (clothbound)

Library of Congress Catalog Card Number: 2006935446
Published by Red Hen Press

The City of Los Angeles Cultural Affairs Department and Los Angeles County Arts
Commission partially support Red Hen Press.

DEPARTMENT OF CULTURAL AFFAIRS
City of Los Angeles

Printed in Canada
First Edition

Author's Note

Ludlow is a work of fiction, but certain characters and events have their origins in historical fact, and several books have been helpful to me as I shaped the story. Among the best are *Buried Unsung: Louis Tikas and the Ludlow Massacre*, by Zeese Papanikolas, and *The Great Coalfield War*, by George S. McGovern and Leonard F. Guttridge. In addition I should mention *La Gente: Hispano Identity and Life in Colorado*, edited by Vincent C. de Baca, as well as the published folklore researches of Professor Rubén Cobos. Portions of this book originally appeared in *The Hudson Review* and *Alabama Literary Review*. I wish to thank the many friends who gave me suggestions about the manuscript, among them Ted Kooser, Zeese Papanikolas, Jim Moore, JoAnn Verberg, Jon Mooallem, Charlotte Innes, Andrew Hudgins, R. S. Gwynn, Owen Cramer and Timothy Murphy. Thanks are also due to the Colorado College and the Hulbert Center for Southwest Studies. My deepest debt is acknowledged in the dedication.

For Paula Deitz
And in memory of Frederick Morgan

CONTENTS

Part One

Part Two

Part Three

Un ciego estaba escribiendo
lo que un mudo decía
y un sordo estaba escuchando
pa platicarlo otro día.

A blind man was writing down
What a deaf-mute was saying,
And a deaf man was listening
In order to talk about it next day.

—folk song collected by Rubén Cobos

. . . ἢ μήπως ὄχι δὲν ἀπομένει τίποτε παρὰ μόνο τὸ βάρος
ἡ νοσταλγία τοῦ βάρους μιᾶς ὕπαρξης ζωντανῆς
ἐκεῖ ποὺ μένουμε τώρα ἀνυπόστατοι λυγίζοντας. . . .

. . . or perhaps no, nothing remains but the weight
the nostalgia for the weight of a living being
where we the ungrounded ones now abide. . . .

—George Seferis,
"The King of Asine"

Part One

1. *La Huerfana*

Shot-firers filed in after the diggers left
and found the marked drills for their measured shot.
As daylight died the men were blasting deep
for the next day's cuts of coal.
                              Down below
the mesa, smells of cooking rose from shacks
in rows, and there Luisa scrubbed the pot
as if she were some miner's wife and not
a sapper's daughter, scrawny, barely twelve.

Some nights she waited till the lamps went out
in cabins all along the line, where men
who'd tried to wash the coal dust from their skin
snored and tossed, endured by wives and children,
catching sleep for an early start—from dark
to dark below,
from desert stars to flickering kerosene,
foul air that made the young men think of death.

Luisa waited in the twilit Babel
of miners bedding down—some Mexican
like her late mother, some filling the night
with songs in Welsh, Italian. Some were Greek
and talked of fighting wars against the Turks
and made *bouzouki* strings and *lyras* sing,
their workers' fingers nimble when they played
in high dry air of a Colorado camp.

But some nights she could barely hear the life
around her, hauling water from the creek
and pouring off the clearer part for drinking,
her heart held steady till explosions came
from gaping mines uphill, dull thudding sounds
like the push of air a man's torso made
when other men lit into him with fists.
The mesa sounded like a beaten man,

pinned down and beaten senseless in the night
the way it sometimes happened to a scab
or union organizer or a man
brought in from far away to agitate.
No one who grew up as Luisa had
in coal camps from Trinidad to Pueblo,
watching the typhoid rake through families,
could say she'd never seen a beaten man.

The mines made widows too, when timbermen
or diggers deep inside the earth cut through
to gas and lanterns set it off, or when
the pillared chambers fell. You heard a slump
within, and some poor digger ran out choking
there was thirty boys still trapped in the seam.
And some days all you'd see was bodies carted
down the hill and bosses counting heads.

—⚮—

Luisa's father was John Mole, the firer,
and on his team were Lefty Calabrini,
who'd lost three fingers of his gnarled right hand,
Cash Jackson, who never saved a penny,
Too Tall MacIntosh, who acquired a stoop
from running wire to the ignition box.
"I've always been a Mole," her father joked
about his boyhood underground in Wales.

He never talked about New Mexico,
Luisa's mother, or the typhoid curse
that took so many from this vale of tears.
He saved to buy a headstone, read his Bible,
always wore a tie to church on Sunday,
taught his child to be polite to strangers
and never say a word against a man
or woman in the camp. Luisa heard

the others whisper when her father passed,
"Now there's a man who knows his dynamite.
There's luck runs in his crew."

                         "He never lost
a single fella worked for him."

                         "But luck
run out at home and took Conchata with it.
Poor man's saddled with that homely girl
to care for."

                 "No, she cares for *him*. She works
her little fingers to the bone, that girl."

And others talked without a single word,
the married men or bachelors who watched
behind her father's back, whose sooty faces
said they saw her body growing underneath
the man's jacket she wore against their stares.
She's not so skinny, their tough faces said.
She's filling out. She has her mother's sway.
All said in silence and behind John Mole.

Luisa learned to walk aiming her eyes
just ahead on the hard ground of the path,
holding two buckets so they wouldn't slosh,
and she could always swing them if some fella
jumped her in the scrub. She kept her eyes peeled
as her father told her, adding this advice:
"Never trust a stranger, child. Some of these
have come from lawless places of the world."

He meant the Greeks. They spoke few English words
and walked like men who looked askance at work,
their olive fingers turning beads, dark eyes
absorbing every gesture of the camp.
Luisa heard their chatter, their *Ella,*
ella koritsáki mou, no safety
in their tone, the plaintive tenor of their songs,
their words a gravel to confound the tongue.

And now the camp fell quiet. Lamps were snuffed.
The beaten man had sighed back into earth
and firing crews descended paths in moonlight,
their gossip happy under summer stars
with all of heaven blue, dark blue above,
a perfect dome from runneled prairies east
to all the coal camps under the Front Range.
And there atop that dome, the Greeks would say,

the eyes of Christ *Pantokrátor*, World-king,
watched all, saw more than J. C. Osgood did
from Redstone or the C. F. & I., saw more
than John Mole tamping down his corncob pipe
and cupping a lighted match against the breeze,
saw more than young Luisa Mole who waited
curled beneath a blanket in her bunk,
hearing the voices of returning men—

saw more, I would imagine, if he lived
as the believers say he did, than barons
hours later in Manhattan, one especially
thinking of Sunday school and frugal sleep,
and of investments in some mines out West,
and that his father, John D., Senior, would
approve the profit and apply the cost
adroitly as before. The will of God.

But the eyes of heaven are no living eyes
as we might picture them, compassionate
or fierce. They are the blankness over all,
beautiful and empty as deep space,
the diamond-hard reflections of the stars.
I know that sky. I come to know it better
year by year, the sky of passing time
that pools and vanishes. I have come back.

—⁂—

I saw this land first in a boyhood dream
made of my father's stories. Colorado,
where the red of earth turned at night to the blue
of moonlit heaven, where coyotes yapped
up the arroyo, and the deer came down
to seek unsullied water in the streams.
It was a fantasy:
cowboys and Indians. *Home on the Range.*

And then I saw it from an uncle's car
on the hot, endless drive from his Boulder home
to Trinidad, before the Interstate
and air-conditioning—in the late fifties.
I, the spoiled middle son of a doctor
asking when we'd get there, wherever *there* was,
and now *there* seemed so inhospitable
I no doubt longed for my rainy home up north.

A solitary cone of rock rose up
from lacerated land, the dry arroyos,
scars that scuppered water in flood season
down to a river. In dusty summertime
the cottonwoods eked out a living there
in a ragged line below the high peaks.
The ground was a plate of stony scutes that shone
like diamonds at noon, an hour when diamondbacks

coiled on sunbaked rocks. Or so I pictured
in color films imagination shot.
The butte they called *El huerfano*, alone
east of the highway. . . . We were driving south,
and to the west the heat-waved mountains rose,
abrasive peaks without a trace of snow,
bare rock above a belt of evergreens.
This was my father's home. My father had

a childhood here, so far away from mine,
and knew of mines in the long-vanished towns,
a butte the Mexicans had named "the Orphan,"
and two peaks Indians called the *Huajatollas*,
"Breasts of the Earth," that made me and my brother
giggle, pounding each other's arms. "Ludlow,"
my uncle said and pointed. Father told
of militia men posted in those hills,

the miners camped below. "The bastards fired
machine guns on the miners' tents," he said.
"Yes, and set the tents on fire"—our uncle
told the rest, but I was much too young
to think of soldiers doing any evil,
and yawned these complications out of mind.
An open window of my uncle's car
with dry wind whooshing through it framed my dreams.

—ɷ—

I dream Luisa dreaming at midday,
picking through heaps of bony by the mine
for any bits of coal to burn in the stove.
She has walked far to gather wood, the land
picked clean for miles around, found water
that runs clean upstream from the Berwind mines,
but it's far to carry such a heavy load.
Luisa carries more than wood and water.

Her dream is simple—a mother-moment
of brushing hair outdoors one summer day.
Her mother told about New Mexico,
el hueso gisandero, how the village
shared the thigh bone of a buffalo,
its marrow flavored broth from every fire
until the magic of the bone was gone
and women cut it into squares for buttons.

Luisa shakes it off. She holds her apron
close to keep the company eyes from spying
the eight small knobs of coal it holds. Her shoes
worn thin as calluses, she sidesteps down
the sliding slag, then takes the path that cuts
across the switchbacked wagon road to home.
The men are at the mines. The firers check
their wire and fuses. Timekeepers keep time

as only timekeepers can. A train goes by
for Trinidad, a town where agitators
hawk their leftist papers and talk of strikes.
At Walsenburg the crooked sheriff, Jeff
"King" Farr, receives an order of new rifles,
while up in Denver Damon Runyon writes
of miners dying in more accidents:
"With gunny sacking spread on the greasy floor

and with tubs and tables ready, the coroner
of Las Animas waits in a grimy machine shop
for the pitiful procession that must soon come
filing out of the dismal hole in the hillside."
Rising from the *Rocky Mountain News*,
the moment juts into the stream of time
where Billy Reno, the company's chief thug,
beats the tar out of nosy journalists.

The agitators wait for union orders.
The managers of pluck me stores await
bankers who will change the miners' scrip
for cash that would enable them to move,
if they are lucky, down to Trinidad.
The rocks outwait the people, rise and fall
so slowly human beings are unaware
even as they dig for their lives within.

All are waiting one summer afternoon,
kept by time like piñon and prickly pear,
like dry wash and cow pie, buffalo skull,
like the man beaten in a world below
the crust of earth where life is standing still.
Luisa Mole arrives at her cabin door
to spill the bits of coal and build the fire
for supper. It will be her father's last.

—∾—

With Too Tall, Lefty, and their partner, Cash,
John Mole had checked the charges, tamped them in
to open an impressive seam, pure coal
beyond the pillars cut that afternoon.
Despite the coal dust on his sleeves, the room
felt clean, well dug and tidy. The black seam,
bituminous, showed crystal facets
that caught the lamplight almost beautifully.

"She's ready, John," said Lefty. They took the spool
between them and ran stooping up the slope
while Too Tall gathered the lamps behind them.
John was nearly forty. His years below
had given him a touch of the black lung
and made him learn the craft of dynamite
for better pay and less time underground.
He couldn't run far before he stopped to cough.

This night he paused so often for some air
that Cash stepped in to heft the spool. "Away,
ye've done enough," said Too Tall with his burr.
"Away with ye. Off ye go." John Mole went up
the path of mules and men, from dark to light,
or light that failed even as it dazzled him.
Coughing to clear his lungs,
he stood still in the failing light, looking down

on lamplit houses far below, and then
the folded, darkening land spreading east.
He knew the others watched him without hate
though measuring his strength against the day
he'd quit. He saw that day and was afraid
but pushed his fear as he had always done
deep into the mine of himself, unquarried
and unspoken of like most other feelings.

"She's wired up, John. She'll take the fuckin plunge."
Lefty passed his stubbed hand above the box
in a crippled benediction, laughing.
They left the tipple for a boulder's shelter.
"Fire below," John said.
                            The first charge rumbled
almost out of ear-shot. The second missed.
"The bitch," said Lefty. "She won't give over."
"Connection's bad," John said. "You lads stay here."

"Sit you down," said Too Tall. "Ye'll have a fit."
"I'm fine," said John Mole. "I can splice a wire."
So he walked upright the way they all had come,
goggles on, a kerchief tied for breathing
dust that had shaken loose in the first blast.
Swallowed in utter dark, he pushed his fear
into that very mine, and took his last steps,
a man dead set to prove he was a man.

—∞—

The coroner knew when they had brought him down
whose stunned remains these were, his limbs intact,
his face the face of a man who only slept,
internal organs jellied by the blast
that knocked him through a thin wall of the mine.
"It finally got John Mole," he said. "Jesus,
I never thought I'd see you bring him in."
And Too Tall MacIntosh was almost crying.

The first explosion cut a vein of gas
that flooded chambers. It was John Mole's lamp
that set it off. "A lucky accident,"
said some, "to kill one man. It could kill fifty."
"He was as good as fifty men," said Cash,
but inside thought it was the end for Mole
before he died. A man worn out for work,
who lost his purpose when he lost his wife.

There was the girl, of course, who ran out screaming
when she heard, and seemed to pummel the earth,
her fists stuck full of cactus spines and bleeding,
her wails heard all that night at a neighbor's hearth.
La huerfana, they called her. *Pobrecita*.
For weeks thereafter she was desolate,
until some company lackey came to tell her
she would have to leave. Her little house was let.

2. *Late Hunting*

Long-legged and agile, the native scrapper
hunting alone or in packs, feasting, starving,
tricking its small prey to leave their burrows,
coyote was no friend to local ranchers.
They shot the beasts and hung their carcasses
as fenceline warnings. Still coyote preyed
by day or night, survival's worshipper,
and skirted camps so humans wouldn't see him.

Sometimes he picked clean what others killed—
the catamounts or men with guns, the blizzards
that left cattle frozen on the prairie
and drove hardscrabble ranchers to despair.
Some sign of death could meet a fellow's eye
wherever he looked: knives in a saloon,
the typhoid spread by dirty water, diggers
buried by the dozen deep in the mines.

Mole's death was one more sadness in the towns:
Tabasco, Berwind, Ludlow, Aguilar. . . .
Las Animas County had *La huerfana*
as yet another cause for discontent.
"It was her father's life," one digger said,
"his twelve years working for the C. F. & I.
The bastards tried to pay her damages
in scrip, then set her packing up the house."

Another shook his head: "Mole should've known.
He should've sat and waited for the Fire-boss
to test for gas. It wasn't safe to go
but he went anyway—his own mistake."
And of the girl, "She still a child," said one.
"She need *familia*. Where she go spend
the paper they give her for the pluck me store?
Now they got strangers in the house with her."

Most kept their voices low or did not speak
for fear of company spies. Too Tall and Lefty
chanced it the afternoon the mine was closed
and walked the dozen miles to Trinidad.
The union man, John Lawson, had come down
from Denver. In a sympathizer's house
he met small groups of men. Big, steady-eyed
as he shook their hands, he had a boxer's build.

He spoke of work as a man who knew work:
"I was a picker back in Pennsylvania,
nine years old and all day climbing the slag.
I've done my share of digging, timber cutting.
I was down here for the strike in '03,
seven years ago. Damn near lost my wife
and daughter when they dynamited our shack.
I took a bullet for the cause. We lost

because they sent militia with their guards
and trained in scabs—new starving immigrants."
He paused, seeming to face each man who stood
in the lamplit room, and for that moment he
was P. T. Barnum and he knew his crowd
by heart. "You boys, maybe you were the scabs?
You needed work and they had work to give?
It starts that way. The scabs take union jobs

and soon enough the scabs learn why we struck.
We'll get no help from William Howard Taft
or Guggenheims and Rockefellers, the New York
money-grubbers. They see you as capital."
And Too Tall thought he'd never heard a man
speak on his feet like this one, who could use
words and fists in equal measure. He smelled
the unwashed bodies of men pressing close

to listen as John Lawson told of fights,
of sneaking into Walsenburg one night
where "King" Farr ran saloons and whorehouses,
ran the county as his own demesne
in fealty to those greater kings back East,
and deputized any man who'd wear a gun
or wield a blackjack on the law's behalf.
Lawson took his lumps there, as did others.

That was how John Lawson worked at first—
in small groups, winning men with words and not
hysterics, careful to talk of fairness, bonds
a working man could understand, the things
he saw himself, from cheating weight men to
the beatings meted out by Sheriff Farr.
The company had eyes in Trinidad
as well, so one man stood watch at the door.

"Our time is coming," he told the men. "Tonight
you see a handful whispering in a room,
but when we shut down every mine, stay clear
of their illegal scrip
and douse coke-oven fires, you bet your life
they'll notice."
                    "We've only scrip," said Too Tall.
"It's company beans we eat or we eat nothing,
company homes or we're in cardboard boxes."

"That's why the union's here. Only in a group,
only together can we win the day."
"They'll fight," said Too Tall, "as they always have."
He thought of his dead friend and had no heart
to see more death.
"And we'll fight back," John Lawson said. "The union
wants a victory and the nation needs it.
We're hoarding guns. Now the job's to win peace."

The fierceness in his face had disappeared.
"Peace among the miners. Stop Piedmontese
from scrapping with Sicilians, keep the Slavs
from back-stabbing Japs, restrain the Greeks
when a Cretan picks a fight.
A regular Mexican riot's what they want.
The company pretends to be paternal,
pretends they give a damn who lives and dies.

They want you tribes of miners to say thanks
for the table scraps they give of their good hearts.
But men, these rich rats are getting fatter
daily on your sweat, your sweethearts' hunger.
Now's the time for an alternative
to pissing your days in someone else's dirt."
Collar loose, sleeves rolled, big hands on hips,
Lawson paced, then looked at Lefty and Too Tall:

"You blasting crews take home a wage—it's scrip
but it's pay by the job. What's a digger get?
He's got a weight man tagging every ton
he wheels out—coal, not slag. He's got to pick
the bony from the coal—that's unpaid dead-work.
And then there's timbers and props to make it safe—
no pay for that so a man just timbers less
with one result—more dead Dagos and Japs,

and what mine owner ever cared for them?"
He thumped his chest. "We're here to say a Jap's
as good as a Mexican Dago Greek
and they're all as good as any Rockefeller.
We want a union. We want an eight-hour day
and the free choice of where to spend cash wages
and fair pay for dead-work. We only ask
what's ours, but if it's war the company wants

we'll find a good use for your dynamite."

—m—

They left the meeting in the predawn dark
and started north. Outside of town they took
the moonlit footpaths cutting the dirt roads.
Lefty seemed to feel in his right hand
a ready fist—who needed fingers to fight?
With each step his mind was naming the names
of men he'd pick for beatings. There was Coyle,
for one, who weighed coal on company scales.

There were diggers like Pacheco, Fante, Smith,
who whispered to bosses what they heard men say
below in the dark. The spies were obvious
because they fried more bacon with their beans
and all their kids wore shoes. He was a scrapper,
Lefty was, and never dodged a fight.
From the day he reached New York at age ten,
he fought hard and he learned American.

Mostly he learned to swear. He had a nose
for women, could sniff a whore out of a pew
(not that he went to church)
and seemed to fight and fuck his way through life
when he wasn't blowing rock walls to bits.
"Do you think we'll do it?' he asked the Scot.
"We could make those bastards piss their britches,
couldn't we? We could bust a few noses."

"Aye," said Too Tall. "We could that. And our own
could bleed a little too. Both sides are scunnered.
They'll make a scrimmage or a heap of bones."
He paused on the footpath, hands in trouser pockets,
and then looked down at Lefty. "I'm afraid
the fight you're looking for will come too soon."
Some movement caught his eye. He turned to look
but it was only moonlight catching glints

of broken glass beside the path. He stared
a long time at night shadows from the scrub.
And though the land was high and dry out here
he thought of Ayrshire where he used to walk
on nights like this, a moon to light the way.
"I wonder," he said. And Lefty answered him:
"That's your trouble, always wondering something."
And Too Tall: "If I'll stay on here, I mean."

"This is my home," said Lefty. "I'll kill the man
who says it isn't. I'll kill him with one hand
if I have to."
                    "No," said his friend. "Not I.
I mean I've no objection to a union,
but I won't kill. And won't stay here forever.
What I want's a cash wage for a day's work,
and one day I'll pack up my wife and boys
and buy a passage home." A wooden snap

made both men stop and look. The four-legged shadow
scooted from behind a tree and crossed
the scrub, a furry critter in its jaws.
"An early breakfast," Too Tall said, and laughed.
"Who knows what's to become of the likes of us?
I wonder every time I set a wire,
and now I wonder what our friend John Mole
would make of all this talk."

Mention of the dead man changed his mood
as if a cloud had crossed the moon, and sight
of that coyote with its pulsing food
darting for cover at the end of night.
He felt so tired and hungry. They stopped to eat
dry bread they'd brought along for the long hike.
"I know," said Lefty as he rubbed his feet.
"He'd go too slow at first. And then he'd strike."

3. *The Pluck Me Store*

Five nights after the firing crew brought word
of his death, John Mole stooped in at the door.
Luisa heard his boots scrape on the boards
and tried to lift her head, but she was held
by fear she couldn't name, lay in her bunk
feeling his presence. She saw him strike a match
and touch it to the oily wick and lean
in lamplight over his sleeping daughter's form.

Her form. Her eyes were open and his face
with black streaks underneath his bushy brows
hovered there. She knew he looked like that,
not burned as you might expect, but suffocated,
crushed and thrown through a wall. "A good death,"
Too Tall said, "but too young." "No death is good,"
said Lefty. "Death's an insult to a man."
And there he was, alive above her bunk

until she bolted, shouting "Papa!" loud
enough to wake the dead—only to find
she was awake and he was dead again,
again, as if each dying made it harder.
Señora Robles moved the cardboard wall
beside her bed. To keep the sobbing girl
from waking others who now shared the house,
she held her shoulders, rocking her back to sleep.

Dreams of her mother were so different,
both day and night: her quiet suffering,
fever and rash. Luisa couldn't believe,
despite the nightdress soaked with sweat, the moans
in Mexican, the panic in her eyes
when Conchata saw her only living child,
what stillness she became one autumn morning,
washed by women while her daughter sobbed.

Gone now as the earth itself was gone
it seemed, days at a time. The piñon jays
that fed amid the scrub—they were not real.
Jackrabbits pausing on a knoll were ghosts
as big as dogs, come for memory's scraps,
the leavings of a life no longer lived.
She heard the neighbors talk: "What can we do?"
Nothing. Nothing. Nothing. Nothing. Nothing.

One day a woman walked up from the train
who said she had Luisa's name in a book
and would explain the orphanage in Pueblo
for miner's children who had lost all kin.
They sat on chairs outside in the dirt yard.
The woman talked—that too no longer real.
Nothing was real except the kindling splinter
Luisa used to scrape a toenail, peeling

oily grit from underneath, wanting
to be clean. She couldn't raise her eyes to look
because to look at the round-faced woman
sweating in her shirtwaist meant she was real
and they were truly dead. She knew only
not to betray them out of their shared life—
the kind man tamping down his corncob pipe,
the wife he cried for till his eyes were red.

The other women gathered to defend her
with Mrs. MacIntosh, Señora Robles.
"She can't stay here," the stranger was explaining.
"I see she isn't eating well, how thin
she is. I have instructions. Others need
her corner of the house. There are others—
workers, families, children. They have jobs.
I have a job. Responsibilities."

Those wiry women swept the stranger off
as swiftly as they could.
 "We've heard about that home. It's far away
from everything she knows. She won't go there
if we can help it."
                    "Lady, write this on
your paper, that we keep the girl with us.
She ours like family. Like child, our own."
Their voices rose, a flock of piñon jays,

and gone was the stranger down the stony path,
gone back to the train, gone back to Pueblo
with her book. Luisa felt familiar hands,
unreal familiar skirts surrounding her.
She watched the sunlight in the risen dust,
a dream of dust choking the dream of summer.
She felt a neighborly caress. "Sweetie,
you sit tight for now. You hear? Sit tight."

"*Arranquera,*" the Señora said. "Hard times."

—∞—

Out of the rockfolds, the scrub, the deep sky,
out of the junipers that loosed the dark
when the sun crept over the mountaintops,
out of the mouths and tipples of the mines
where men still worked, inquest or no inquest,
where coke ovens glowed a stone inferno,
out of the train that wailed to Trinidad
and back to Denver with its load of news

came the sound that was not a sound, a muted
scratching for life. All day she watched the hens
of mining families cluck about the houses,
named them by the way they worried or bossed.
One was Mrs. for her Scottish talent,
catching bugs on the ground, one Señora
for the way she pushed the other hens about
despite a tattered wing—coyote plucked.

And the old cock who croaked his song at sunrise
was a Welshman for the way he tried to sing.
Her playthings. Better for not being people
and being so much smaller when they died.
Girls came by, showed her their stitched dolls. Boys looked
over their shoulders, whispered among themselves.
She heard them talking. Breezes. Hens. Women.
Whenever she passed the yards, their washtubs,

their bodies at work. "She knows," said Mrs. "She knows
the rag, the blood. She's not too young for it.
We've men who'd stoop to the wrong thing here.
She isn't safe." And more she wouldn't hear,
though it came at her in whispers from all sides
in the feeding and breeding and dying life of the camp.
She watched as a woman scooped up a hen
by the legs, stepped on its squawking head, and jerked.

—⚏—

"*Casamiento de pobres, fábrica
de limosneros.*" A marriage of the poor
is a factory of beggars.
Señora Robles said it like the scripture,
watching her own young ruffians at play.
She turned back to the stoop where Luisa sat
beside two apple crates of her possessions.
La pobrecita—always waiting for men.

Luisa watched the others watching her
as she had done at her father's funeral,
the short march of neighbors to the dry hill
of wooden markers, words of kindness spoken
for the girl a good man left behind.
He's gone. He's gone. Don't look. Don't ever look.
Señora Robles cooked food like her mother's
with jalapeños and black beans, while Too Tall

on occasion brought a rabbit home for stew.
She hated evenings when he went to work
as her father had, taking the path up
while Robles and his diggers limped back down.
She noticed Mrs. MacIntosh would keep
her thin hands busy as she could to calm
her mind—even that sinewy Glaswegian
who had borne two living children was afraid.

Her boys were Tom and Nicky, eight and six,
and neither of them much help to their mother.
They wore the holes she spent her spare time darning.
Luisa watched them, kept them from snakes
and blasting caps. She carried water, wood
and hunks of scavenged coal. She tried to help
the neighbors who helped her as best she could,
read from her father's Bible, scrubbed their pots.

Too Tall had said her future was arranged
and everyone was safe—what did he mean?
Why did the older women watch her so
and chase the boys away with angry words
in Mexican or Scots, brandishing sticks
to wave them off? She waited on the stoop,
her skirted knees held close as if to guard
her body from the eyes. What wasn't said.

Word reached the pluck me store in Cedar Hill,
where Mrs. Reed, who had four daughters, lay
pregnant, confined to bed by a company doctor.
She'd lost a son last year and couldn't bear,
they said, to lose another.
She had a four-room clapboard house, a well
for water, space beside the kitchen stove
where a thing as slight as young Luisa Mole

could throw a pillow and her blankets down
to sleep. In time perhaps they'd build a bunk.
The girl could cook, clean house and mind the children
in exchange for shelter in a Christian home.
It was arranged. While others crammed her house
Luisa waited with her boxed-up goods
beside her as the buckboard wagon drew
nearer on the road.

She saw the man who drove, his straw hat shading
half his face. She saw Too Tall MacIntosh
on foot beside the wagon, talking to
the man, the straw hat nodding, coat and tie
though it was hot—her future coming close.
The enemy, or so she used to think,
a man of scrip and heavy prices, cursed
by mining folk. A stranger. Mr. Reed.

"Luisa." Too Tall stooped to touch her hair.
"Lass, this man's your new employer. Chin up.
Let's look at you." She saw the man's good shoes
when he stepped down, the trousers, buttoned vest.
"George Reed," said Mr. Reed. "Don't be afraid."
He swung his hat off, a man of thirty years
with blue eyes and a blond mustache, his hair
parted almost down the middle. "That's it,

good girl." His mustache bristled when he smiled.
"She's not much older'n mine. You say she can read?"
"She's had it hard," said Too Tall.
                              "There's plenty
around here's had it hard," said Mr. Reed.
"But we could use the help if she can work.
You can work, can't you, young lady? Luisa,
right? Luisa, you can work, can't you?"
Luisa nodded. "That a girl. Good girl."

They loaded up her apple crates of clothing,
Bible, the wooden *santo* her mother brought
from a village far away, the carver's name
made shiny by the rub of hands: *abuelo*.
"*No tiene uno ni madre*," said
a voice behind her. "Good lass. Good lassie."
"Work hard and don't forget us," said Mrs.
"Good-bye," said the house, the hens, the risen dust.

4. *The Greek-American*

Ilias Spantidakis lay awake
in the narrow bed behind his *kafeneíon*,
thinking of gunfire. Somewhere shuffling feet
and coughing, not his father, not *Babá*—
Gus Kutsofes had got up to stir the fire
and heat the little *bríki* on the stove.
This was Denver. The year was 1912.
Today his fellow Greeks would go to war.

Den eímai Romaíos, eímai Kritikós.
I'm not a Greek, I am a Cretan, though
I'm far away from home. *Ap' to horió.*
Each day this inner dialogue, the boy
he became in dreams reborn an immigrant,
rechristened Louis Tikas in New York,
hopping the westbound freight—Chicago, Denver,
everywhere Greeks said he could find a job.

Some days this waking to himself became
unbearable, like some ill-fitting mask,
the words he'd learned of English hard to hold,
his village dialect a refuge from
estranging streets. How long, O Lord, how long
must one man journey till he finds his home?
But home was Loutra, poverty, the house,
the olive press, his father serving coffee.

And Crete in Limbo, as the Scholar said—
a customer who came to read, to take
a glass of water with his coffee, and,
as he told Louis, hear the accent of
his youth. "Will you go back?" the Scholar asked.
"What would you do there? Live among the brigands?
The bread you make from stones is heavy bread,
my boy. You must cultivate your learning."

How the Scholar lived he had never learned.
His clothes were like a dandified beggar's
and each day he took his corner table
hours at a time for the price of one coffee.
"You have a brain, my boy. You're good at English.
Everybody knows you—the boy who writes."
"I wrote my declaration," Louis said,
"to be a citizen. I signed the papers."

"Yes, but the name you signed was not your own,"
the Scholar answered. He wiped his spectacles
and perched them on his nose. "I know you, my boy.
American—you're so American,
I can tell you dream of silver dollars, eh?
You write your declaration, tell the man
that you intend to be American,
but you dream of going back."

"And you? That book you always read—what is it?
Dante, the Italian, always Dante.
Tell me—are you out of Hell yet?"
                                        "Oh yes,
my boy, I've crossed the river."
                                        "Tell me, then,
about this river. I've crossed a river too,
the Mississippi. Like you I crossed the sea.
But unlike you, I work."
At that he took his rag and wiped the table.

He had such eloquence at morning, before
he rose and pulled his trousers on. It was
a language of his own, a fluency
he never matched aloud, though he had pride
in what he had accomplished. All Greek Town
knew him, the bootblack who became a merchant.
"Now take that document and go to Tikas.
He can read it for you." That's what they said.

Go to Tikas. Go to Tikas, Louis.
And he said his new name as he practiced
signing it, over and over. Twenty-six,
five foot eight, one hundred fifty pounds.
Louis Tikas, merchant, Market Street.
Levéntis. Palikári. Tell the Sultan
Louis Tikas has come to pay a call.
Then Gus poked through the curtain—"You up yet?"

—⚏—

And Crete in Limbo. That was far away
like voices drowning in the sea, still calling.
Gunfire, and a massive Turk collapsed,
spilling his turban on the bloody stones.
When he was three a Loutra man was hanged
from the plane tree in the square. Had he seen
this thing or only heard of it from his father?
When he was ten he saw the burning trees.

1896. The Turks had come
on foot, on horseback: rifles, bayonets
and torches. They burned the churches at Pyghí
where Ilias studied in the secret school
with Father Nicholas. They burned the trees
and wrecked the olive harvest for that year.
The siege at Réthymnon, where Moslems starved,
the Christians slaughtered at Iráklion—

two years of civil war. Then Crete was free!
A Greek, Prince George, was High Commissioner,
and came to feast in nearby villages.
Ilias Spantidakis walked the streets
of Réthymnon, saw Russian soldiers in
their brilliant uniforms, and somehow knew
this was the Limbo Crete the Scholar meant,
protectorate of European powers.

He couldn't hate the foreigners who came,
and they were Orthodox. The refugees
were terrible to see. The *muezzin*
no longer called from the city's minarets,
though there were Moslems still who had not left,
abused by Russian soldiers in the streets.
Ilias took the footpath back to Loutra,
making a vow that he would never kill.

His father's musket hung above the fireplace
till days when he hunted birds on the mountainside
and took Ilias with him. "Learn to shoot,"
his father said. "Here's the lead and powder. Load
from the muzzle, tamp it down, aim and fire."
That musket butted like a Russian cannon
and scattered feathers over a stony field.
He'd killed a falcon, and he felt like crying.

—w—

The smell of eggs in olive oil. Louis,
not Ilias, rose and dressed, in worsted,
not in boots and breeches. He drew the curtain,
nodded to the older man. *San mátia,*
like eyes, the egg yolks sputtered in their whites.
"*Megáli 'méra,*" Gus said. A great day.
"Soon we'll all be Greeks. Greek-Americans.
Whatever we want. Today we eat like kings."

He tipped the *bríki,* filling Louis's cup
with heavy coffee he had ground himself.
"Your turn to sit. A man from Corinthos
will serve you breakfast, eh? You want to smoke?
I made four cigarettes—they're on the table.
Here, feast on a pair of eyes. Remember
this day, October 25th, we're brothers,
Cretan and Corinthian, we're all Greek."

"Yes," said Louis, soaking a rusk in oil
and yolk, "but we had to come to America
to make it happen."
                    "*Ela,*" Gus said. "*Ela
paidí mou.* With your man Venizelos
it will happen soon. We'll have *Enósis.* Crete
is Greek."
          "You mean Greece is Cretan, don't you?
Anyway, we're all Americans."
Louis wiped the egg from his black mustache.

Eleutherios Venizelos watched
from the framed wall photograph, a Cretan hero,
and across the narrow room so dimly lit
by the front window and one electric bulb,
the bearded Patriarch was watching too.
A flag and crucifix were all they had
besides these photographs for decoration,
a stove, six tables, sawdust on the floor,

a case in which they kept the bread and olives,
some curtained shelves for plates, a money box
and writing implements, a broom, two aprons.
They were merchants, partners in free trade,
citizens of Greek Town. At eight o'clock
they had a customer. Frayed but dignified,
the Scholar took his customary chair
and said in Greek he'd heard the talk of war.

—◊—

Ilias Spantidakis was nineteen
when Venizelists rose against the Russians.
The men of Loutra heard the call, went out
to guard their olive trees, then joined *andártes*
from the White Mountains, booted men with beards
and muskets. At Atsipopoulo he fired
his father's gun for the first time at a man
and heard the soldier screaming for his God.

A failed revolt, but he had learned to fight.
And now, October 25th, Louis stood
amid the crowd of Greeks on Champa Street,
hearing talk of war in Macedonia.
Four hundred Greeks would board the special train
then sail for home to save the Fatherland
against the Turks. With Gus he'd closed the shop
and joined the current of the multitude.

The Colorado sky, bluer than the flag
of Greece, spread almost cloudless over Denver,
city of cooking fires and crowded streets,
of cattle pens, cowboys and derelicts,
the whores and immigrants in their Sunday best.
Behind the fresh recruits, a marching band,
the clergy and the flags.
In all his six years in America,

living by his wits, his love of mankind
even when Yanks or Greeks were cheating him,
Louis never felt so proud, so desolate—
almost a Greek, almost American.
He joined those marching in the big parade
who would stay behind but wished their brothers well.
They were a crowd, an army with two flags.
He looked for friends among the heads and hats,

perhaps Dimitris, whom he knew in Crete,
the gigolo who never found a woman,
who found Ilias in the harbor street
at Réthymnon, and took his elbow, saying,
"Look, my friend. Look at the Cretan boys
who dive among the ships for any coin
the sailors toss. Look at the rags we wear.
How will your sisters make a dowry here?

How long will it take you, how many years
before you walk like a free man in Greece?
You're good at school, my friend, good-looking, too.
How many decades will it take until
you can afford to marry? Look at the girls
even in Réthymno, the young ones married
to rich old men with spittle on their chins.
Look at their suffering. Look at their sad eyes.

Now look beyond the fishing caiques—you see?
The ship *Dareios*, bound for Patras harbor.
That's where you find ships to America
where everybody has a job. The women
in America will fuck a handsome boy
for nothing. Money flows like water—rivers
of money. A President named Rockefeller
gives you a job the moment you disembark."

Yes, Dimitris, always dreaming, believed
that bastard, Louis Skliris, and took a job
on the road to Cripple Creek, a job he paid for
only to find that no job had existed.
He was back in Denver. Louis rarely saw him.
One day he came into the coffee shop
with schemes about the coal fields to the north.
"*Oneiro*," said Louis. "A dream. Someone's lying."

But other men who gossiped in the shop
were talking about coal. When there were strikes
mine owners hired scabs, gave them houses.
It was dirty work, but say you worked six months
and didn't spend your pay on whores or poker.
Say you hid your money in a box
and say you made more money speaking English
to the bosses, Greek among the immigrants.

Say you could live a life of discipline,
I know it isn't human but say you could.
There would be money for your sisters' dowries,
money even for a picture bride
direct from Greece.
                              And so his mind ran on
long after the parade, when he returned
through strangely quiet streets, unlocked the door
and let the straggling customers back in.

Till midnight all the talking was of war,
the Scholar in the midst of it, performing
feats of intellect, accepting the smokes
Gus offered him to keep him speaking. War?
With the Ottomans? A dying empire's troops
Would never stand up to the Greeks, but Greeks
were fools. Constantinopoli? He tapped
his temple. A city only of the mind.

At that the fights erupted. Louis played
his customary role of making peace
and bade his countrymen good night. And after
Gus had gone to bed he locked the shop
and walked down Market Street. He knew the houses
he was looking for, the mood of restlessness
that meant he needed company, though shame
at spending money for a woman wracked his brain.

—m—

This singular man. This footnote nearly lost
from pages of the history books. Louis-
Ilias, named for the fiery prophet,
but often so uncertain of his skin
that only someone else's touch, some whore
who thought he was Sicilian or a Serb,
and took the money first and said no kissing,
made him believe that he was truly alive. . . .

What does it mean—nation of immigrants?
What are the accents, fables, voices of roads,
the tall tales told by the smallest desert plants?
Even the wind in the barbed wire goads
me into making lines, fencing my vagrant thought.
A story is the language of desire.
A journey home is never what it ought
to be.
      A land of broken glass. Of gunfire.

5. *Recalled to Life*

"Your name's Luisa?" Mrs. Reed had sat
propped up with pillows on her bed,
her eyes inquisitive and kind, long hair
fanned about her shoulders. "Don't be afraid.
Come in. Sorry I have to lie abed.
Mr. Reed won't hear me contradict
the doctor. Doesn't matter that I feel
just fine except I'm bigger than a barn."

She took Luisa's hand, made room for her
to sit on the high mattress. "Young lady,
you'll be a help, I swear. You've met the girls,
I see. They're wild, but I've a feeling that
won't bother you. I see it in your eyes."
Mrs. Reed's were lighter than Luisa's,
her skin lighter, reddened at the knuckles
by housework, her wavy auburn hair so clean

it made Luisa feel like a dried-up stick
they'd picked up in the coal dust and brought home,
her own skin dark and callused, paler where
the loose sack of her dress had covered it.
Mr. Reed had made her take a bath
in the kitchen tub before she met his wife,
and she had been afraid, but now she sat
so high her feet were off the floor, and looked

at this kind woman's hands. The room was cool
and clean, with curtains on the one window,
cupboards for hanging clothes, a deal dresser
with a wooden box on top, two or three
of a man's collars lined up next to it.
"Now tell me about yourself," said Mrs. Reed.
"I understand you're partly Mexican
but had an English father? You can read?"

Luisa didn't dare correct her. Welsh
was almost English, anyway, and English
the language she knew best, though her mother
spoke it brokenly. She tried to answer
but there was too much weight within her chest
as she fought back tears. "There there, Luisa.
No need to talk right now. I know the grief
you've had. These things are hard, and we've all had them."

How could it be? How could the beautiful
and still-young mother clasping Luisa's hand
have known—first the typhoid, then the explosion?
She tightened her lower lip but couldn't stop
its trembling, couldn't raise her eyes for fear
they'd fill with tears. "All right, young lady.
Why don't you find those savages I've raised
and have them show you where the food is kept?"

There was so much to learn about the house,
its other bedroom for the girls, kitchen
with cookstove, cupboards, window, and a sink
with a pump handle that brought the water in,
out back a privy with a door. So much
for only six with one more on the way.
There were two upholstered chairs, electric lights,
a second little stove just for the parlor.

And books! On a parlor shelf the volumes
leaned in their cloth jackets, Shakespeare, Dickens,
and someone called Longfellow who would be,
Luisa thought, as tall as Too Tall was.
She touched the golden letters on their spines
the moment she saw them, and the oldest girl
named Daisy said of course she could read them.
"You're s'posed to read to us when Mommy's tired."

Daisy, seven and severe, had no nickname.
Elizabeth was Libby. She was six.
Next came Martha—Marty—who was five,
and Katherine—Casey—of course was four.
The girls had greeted her in smocks and knee socks,
their faces smudged from playing in the dirt,
their blonde hair bound with ribbons they tied themselves
at crazy angles, giggling, rushing about.

Mr. Reed had gone to the store to work
with his brother, and the girls took Luisa's hands
to show her all four rooms of the house, the shelves
of cans. Daisy opened the icebox door
to show her the salt-pork wrapped in paper.
"You're s'posed to boil potatoes with the pork
for supper, and tomorrow you bake bread
and we get to help. The dough has to rise."

"And you have to knead it!" shouted Libby.
"Like this!" said Marty, making a little fist.
"Knead, knead, kneadity deed," said Casey, turning
circles like a dervish on the wood floor.
"Simmer down," their mother shouted from
her room. "You'll be the death of me, I swear.
Luisa, start 'em playing a game outside
and then get to the supper. Daisy, let

the poor girl work. The men will be home soon."

—∞—

Two years had passed among this family.
Luisa had new clothes and shoes, a bunk
for sleeping built into the kitchen wall.
That first fall little George was born. The girls
would call him Pud, but never felt the need
to tell her where they got that name. Now Pud
was nearly two, confused, always underfoot,
sucking his dirty thumb.

The Reeds were always working, always dashing
on some forgotten errand. The telephone
inside the shop would ring, and Mr. Reed
would hitch the wagon, racing down the hill
to meet an order coming on the train.
His younger brother, Arthur, worked the counter,
and often joined the family for meals.
And Mrs. Reed could navigate the storm

of children, cooking, laundry, giving orders
and stitching a heap of clothes, holding three
conversations at once without ever
losing her temper, though often she looked thin
and had the coffee jitters.
She kept a pot warm on the stove, and drank
more than the men. She shot through a day's work
until she nodded off before the children.

When Arthur came to dinner the men talked
prices for flour and bacon, bullets, boots.
They ran a regular mercantile, and had
to keep the prices high, they said, or lose
all chance to profit for themselves. "A man's
initiative is all he's got, he can't
give all to the C. F. & I., now, can he?"
"We're middle-men," said Arthur. "We feel the pinch."

And Mr. Reed would nod agreement, adding
they would have to get out before too long.
Their supper finished, the two brothers sat
while Daisy cleared the table, Luisa washed,
and Mrs. Reed picked up her mending basket,
minding the chatter of the younger children.
"The thing I hate's these immigrants who don't
know how to tell you what they want," said Arthur.

"Some of them go empty-handed. You write
the prices down and they get all confused
and leave without a purchase, walk all the way
to Berwind where they come from. What I think is
the company should give them English lessons."
"Who's got the time for that?" said Mr. Reed.
"We're here to do a service, but we've got
problems of our own. The other day

they hired more guards to stop the miners thieving.
Know how they make them legal to wear guns?
Get them a license to be game wardens, see,
like something Sheriff Farr in Walsenburg
would do. The thing is, everybody here
is free to get around the law. The law
out West is see what you can get away with.
These immigrants know damn well how it works."

And sometimes Arthur looked Luisa's way,
and made some comment about the Mexicans
or Wops, and said to Mrs. Reed, "I'm sorry,
Sarah, but you don't even want to know
the kind of animals they hire. There's killings
in those camps. There's thieves who would slit your throat
as soon as look at you. They say the Greeks
are worst, but some of the Wops are just as bad."

And one day in a game of blindman's buff
Luisa played when she had finished chores
she heard the girls discussing Wops and Chinks,
Japtown and Greektown, and as they chattered
they looked her way as if to test their words,
and she knew she was only sometimes part
of their family circle. Though Mrs. Reed
was always kind, kindness was not the same

as blood or love. She was still a Mexican.
Or was it that? Was it her darker skin,
her Indian blood, or only that she came
from the houses lined up in the canyon,
closer to the turmoil of the hills,
the shifts of miners, masons, timber men,
the noise and smoke? That night she couldn't sleep,
remembering her neighbors in the camp.

—⚹—

Most days the work soaked up the passing hours
with baking, cleaning, laundry, taking the girls
downhill to school and sometimes staying there
to help the company teacher, Mrs. Carter,
or just to linger and absorb new knowledge,
numbers or geography or reading.
Some afternoons she joined the girls at play
behind the store, climbing an old barrel,

searching the shed and scrub for any eggs
the hens had laid. They were allowed long walks
behind the store, up to the mesa's summit
where they heard the clamor, saw the fire and smoke
from up the canyon, counted cars of trains
that passed between them and the low Black Hills.
It was a home, chaotic to be sure,
but mostly welcoming. When snows blew in
George Reed came home with a crate of black boots
and sat in the heated parlor while they tried them on.

That spring, in 1912, Luisa stood
sweeping the front porch of the pluck me store
one day, hearing a coughing motorcar
come up the muddy track. It wheezed and rattled
and almost didn't make it, tires spinning,
but finally it stopped beside the steps.

Two men got out in suits and bowler hats,
scowling at the mud beneath their shoes.
They had red faces, and where their jackets opened
she saw they carried pistols in their gunbelts.
Maybe they were the law. They tipped their hats
at her and stepped inside.
                                    That night after supper
she washed the dishes and let Daisy dry
and Libby stack them in the painted cupboard,

then told the girls to gather in the parlor
for a book. Mrs. Reed was darning socks,
her husband having gone back to the store
with his cigar. Something was different,
something said between the Reeds, some worry.
She'd only heard him say, "I don't like
the look of them." A tone he took when miners
loitered about the stoop as if to rob him.

They kept a rifle in the house, Winchester,
wooden stock and heavy barrel leaning
in the parlor closet. Luisa knew
that Mrs. Reed knew how to use it, saw her
run for it more than once when trouble lurked
about the house, and as she read aloud
she felt it just beyond the door, as if
it leaned upon her brain, and on the words:

The king is kind, and well we know the king
Knows at what time to promise, when to pay.
My father and my uncle and myself
Did give him that same royalty he wears;
And when he was not six and twenty strong,
Sick in the world's regard, wretched and low,
A poor unminded outlaw sneaking home,
My father gave him welcome to the shore.

It was a history play. They all took parts,
hearing the rage of Hotspur at the king
who came to power after murdering
another king. And Mrs. Reed explained
that it was England and long, long ago,
and things were better in America
without a king who sent his henchmen out
to do such work. But maybe this was hard

and they should find another book to read?
Luisa opened Dickens, which had pictures
and voices she could imitate, so like
some people she had known in her other life.
It was the best of times, it was the worst
of times, it was the age of wisdom, it was
the age of foolishness, it was the epoch
of belief, it was the epoch

of incredulity, it was the season
of Light, it was the season of Darkness,
it was the spring of hope, it was the winter
of despair, we had everything before us,
we had nothing before us, we were all going
direct to Heaven, we were all going
direct the other way. . . . "Well." Mrs. Reed
set down her needles and her yarn. "I guess

there's no avoiding trouble in those books!"

—⚉—

That summer, when Luisa turned fourteen,
the family took her on the southbound train
to Trinidad. The car was full of people
in their best clothes, eating, smoking, pointing
to the bluish steps and far-off tabletop
of Fisher's Peak. They rounded the bend at Forbes
where crowds of immigrants were marching toward
the canyon with its mine. *The best and worst,*

Luisa thought, *so maybe nothing changes.*
Like the day when Too Tall walked up to the store
to buy some fuse—they had run out and sent
for more that wouldn't come until tomorrow—
and stood there with his hat off, hair pressed flat
with sweat, talking only to Mr. Reed
while she was right there stocking shelves. And she
had not known what to say

but cried out anyway, "Mr. MacIntosh!"
And how the blush of pleasure crossed his face,
making him stammer, "Lass, ye've grown so much
I hardly knew ye." And how she'd known right then
it wasn't fuse he wanted, but to see her
and convey his wife's regards and tell her
all was well, or mostly well, in the shacks
with Mrs., and the boys, Señora Robles. . . .

"Of course there's more new families all the time,
more folk who don't know proper English."
The latter said as much for Mr. Reed
and Arthur, meaning, *I'm one who knows his place.*
"I hear some grumbling," said Mr. Reed,
"talk of agitators. I've seen more guards."
"Aye," said Too Tall, "well, I wouldn't know.
I keep my muzzle out of politics."

And how before he left he touched her hair
and wished her well, and she could hardly stand
to see him go but also hardly stand
to have him mixing with the Reeds like that.
Among the immigrants at Forbes she saw
whole families lugging their worldly goods,
men at tables taking names. Then the car
had turned, the mesa had cut off her view.

What was it made the heat rise in her cheeks?
Some shame she felt at being intimate
with all those strangers, knowing what they felt
and knowing she could never tell the Reeds?
It was so hard to have a secret life
beyond the secrets Mrs. Reed had known
and helped her with, the whispers about men
and blood and private dangers. Torn in two

by what she saw both far and near, outside
herself and deep inside, as if to witness
feelings she could never speak aloud,
Luisa knew that something of herself
was gypsy and untouchable and never
to be saved. The birthday dress they promised her
because they were the Reeds and they were kind
was something she would never quite deserve.

—∽—

In Trinidad they strolled Commercial Street
as it wound downhill to the riverbank.
Some streets were dirt, this one paved with red bricks
stamped with the town's name, and jammed with people,
wagons, horses, cars. They looked in windows,
paused to watch the masons cutting stone,
the window washers at the bank, a man
who tried to beat his horse for misbehaving. . . .

Beside the river Mr. Reed declared
it had the longest name of any river
he had known: *"El Rio de las Animas
Perdidas en Purgatorio*—The River
of Lost Souls in Purgatory—a mouthful,
ain't it? Goes back to the conquistadors.
Some got killed by Indians in a raid,
so the river's haunted by them. So they say."

Already Casey and Marty were dragging sticks
in the muddy water, and overhead
the giant cottonwoods were swaying leaves
as if to fan them. They saw an Indian
walk by in his *sarape*, a group of men
burst laughing out of a nearby tavern,
a family in dustcoats, hats and goggles
crossing the plank bridge in a motorcar.

"Well," said Mr. Reed, turning to his wife
and tipping his straw hat back on his head,
"should I tell 'em?" Daisy and Libby took
his hands and tugged. "Tell us what, Daddy,
tell us what?" And just then it was like
the street had turned, no more than half an inch,
and there were all the Reeds becoming one
small circle while Luisa stood outside.

"Yes," said Mrs. Reed," no harm in telling."
Luisa held the stroller where Pud slept
and watched the gathering Reeds,
their nervous vigor and their happiness.
"Well, sometimes hard work comes to something good."
He turned to Mrs. Reed, who said, "You're hopeless.
Children, what he means is that we're moving.
By September we'll be living here in town."

Squealing with delight, the four girls hopped
about like birds in a downpour. Luisa
stared into the buggy at Pud's round face
and felt the city whirl around that space
as she became another nameless creature
on an empty road. But there was Mrs. Reed's
hand on Luisa's hand: "Of course we hoped
you'd move with us, young lady." Small brown weeds

poked from the bricks. Luisa stared as if
she might deserve this luck. Recalled to life.

Part Two

Interlude: January 15, 2003

By now you've guessed this story's partly mine.
I'm forty-eight years old, a college teacher
southbound on the Interstate. Three years
of drought and wildfire summers, little snow,
and high winds lift the topsoil in dark clouds.
All Pueblo huddles in the grit, its mill
a relic of a bygone era, stacks
rust-colored in the dusky blue of sky.

At eighty miles an hour, I seem to force
my aging Subaru against the wind,
then south across Apache Creek until
Huerfano Butte, that isolated cone
of black rock, juts beyond the smoking semis.
Now to the west the Huajatollas rise,
imposing, rocky, veined with ice. I move
into a lost familiarity,

and take the back road into Aguilar,
named for the lookout of its piney bluff.
Shift down, go slow past yards of wrecked cars,
cartwheeling tumbleweed, dry rabbit brush
and leafless trees. A town of broken houses,
though at noon the Sunset Tavern's open.
Slow-moving women shop at Ringo's Market
where I find a copy of *Hispania News*.

An arbitrary route, but it will do
for traveling in time as well as space.
The road winds west along the Apashapa,
that flows in sunlight, freezes in blue shade.
Then snowpack on a washboard road, or mud
where light cuts through the gaps in rocky woods.
At the closed post office of Gulnare, I pause
to check the map, wheel down the narrow road

southeast through leaning fences, double-wides,
along the tree-edged Canyon del Agua track,
number 44.0, toward Ludlow.
A journey made on paper many times before,
but new, and somehow moving as I near
the opening of mesas onto prairie,
the gravel intersection, monument
with statue, plaques and testimonials.

This is where it happened. There's the flat
where striking miners pitched their tents, the pit
protected by a chain-link fence as if
even now the dead were under guard.
There the gaping ruins of a stone saloon,
the shuttered schoolhouse. The road to Berwind
and Tabasco passes under Cedar Hill.
The railbed passes, raised like an old scar.

Even here, even in these haunted canyons,
people come to speculate in land.
They promise houses where the concrete ruins
and sandstone walls with tidy buttresses
are terrible to anyone who knows
their story. *Who could bear to live here now,*
I wonder, *with this weight of shattered dreams?*
Yet people do. People can live anywhere.

The ovens, once an aquaduct of fire,
are smothered by an avalanche of slag.
I climb the sliding hill among juniper
and pine, then take my sandwich from a bag,
my bottled water, a ruminative meal,
sitting on needled ground. The cold wind whirs
among the topknots overhead. I feel
a presence where no other human stirs.

This much is true. I made this trip alone,
my wife and cats back home in Woodland Park.
My sweater stuck with needles, hair wind-blown,
I found a small motel before the dark
closed over Trinidad, and wrote these lines.
My ancestors were business folk who ran
a pluck me store. They visited the mines,
moved on to hopes and failures of their own.

Their lives are part of my life's inventory;
my role grows smaller when I glimpse the whole.
Today I pocketed a lump of coal.
These are the facts, but facts are not the story.

6. *Escape from Underground*

There are photographs and there are books,
the best by Papanikolas, who found
more because he sought more—in libraries,
in voices of the old. All are dead now
who saw what Louis Tikas did at Ludlow;
Zeese Papanikolas heard the rambling men
who patched their memories, stitching the rags
of hearsay, myth, and resurrected desire.

These and the touched-up photos of the time
are, with varied testimony, what we have.
We piece together Tikas as we make
our own past from what evidence we find.
Imagination's arrogance is all
I bring to this, a storyteller's hope
of touching life in others, a poet's love
of tropes and cadences, the sway of words.

Because this story hooks into desires
I've always felt to know the land I come from,
Tikas is one figure I summon back.
Because I lived in Greece, I once reversed
his journey, hoped to find my life abroad
and failed, though not for any lack of love,
I know the salt and brilliance of his sea,
the heat that stuns you, the cicadas' whir,

the bite of *ráki* on a lover's tongue. . . .

—⚎—

From the naked bed of a Denver whore
named Alice—weazened and tubercular—
Ilias Spantidakis moved back in
to his American skin and his new name,
from leading man in Greek to character
in English who confused the tenses, lost
the proper names for abstract principles
and left some articles to faith. Tikas.

Louis. "Louie the Greek" who did not go
to war, who drifted through another day
of making coffee, talking, selling sweets
and reading newspapers for immigrants:
tales of strikes in Utah copper mines—
gun-toting Cretans opened fire at scabs.
Dimitris came, but took no coffee, held
a paper he had brought for Louis to read.

"This says you have a job at the Frederick mine,
Weld County," Louis said. "They pay your train."
"That's what they told me," said Dimitris. "Tools
and housing for all workers who break the strike.
Once you get in they keep you safe from unions,
let you earn your money.
Nothing to spend it on up there—you save
the wages and you buy your passage home."

Louis took a chair to think it over.
First there was Dimitris—always dreaming—
and contracts from Americans always lied.
Then there was the way his body felt,
the dampness of the whore all over him
beneath his shirt. His far off father's voice
that came in letters hinting that more money
might just save the family from ruin.

What am I doing, sitting here like this?
I could grow old here, sweeping old sawdust,
talking to men who are growing old
without pride or women.
He stood and called to Gus. The two men talked,
smoking, arm in arm—a verbal contract
in which Louis could leave his suitcase here,
his Cretan costume and boots, to try the mines.

A matter of percentages and trust—
each man would take a share in the other's work,
and so had nothing to lose. They shook hands,
slapped each others' backs. "If only we had
a little glass of *ráki* for a toast,"
said Louis. But Denver was a dry town.
Dry too the irony of the Scholar's voice
when he saw Louis wadding up his apron:

"My boy, what have you done? What have you done?"

—᠎᠎—

November 9th brought news to the coffee shop.
The Scholar wore his threadbare coat upon
his shoulders in the heated room, and waved
a wire received by one of his companions.
"I have news," he said in Greek, his spectacles
becoming wet with tears as he read aloud:
"November 8, 1912. Salonica
has fallen to the Greeks. The Turks retreat!"

A cheer went up. More Greeks came in to see
what all the fussing was about, and Gus
Kutsofes hugged the Scholar, kissed his cheeks,
demanded silence while the wire was read
half a dozen times, each time to cheers
and then to songs, the words of Solomos,
and finally to dances in a ring,
the chairs and tables pushed back to the walls.

—⫘—

By that time Louis Tikas was in hell
or, as he muttered to his fellow Greeks
crouched in the dark, digging in its direction.
The train unloading men at the Frederick mine
had passed through camps of strikers, barbed wire gates
where guards with gunbelts and long rifles stood,
keeping the union out, the poor scabs in.
A clutch of shacks inside the fence, a scar

of black earth gaping in the low hill's side,
a crowd of pickers, diggers of all ages,
nationalities, the rails for trundling
coal, the flumes for loading trains—all within
the bustling, pounding, smoky, hacking compound
where generators whined, electric lights
on long wires flickered in the gloom. Each day
men rose in darkness in their crowded shacks,

and those who worked in seams the bosses hosed
hoped that their socks and sweaters had dried out.
All life was lived inside the wire, as if
self-sentenced to a concentration camp—
those compounds British soldiers had invented
for the Boers. But here were Greeks, Italians,
Slavs, black slaves' descendents trained from the South
to work in black-face equally with others. . . .

The first day Louis Tikas hauled a pick
beneath the earth, smelling sweat and mule shit,
kerosene and dust, he felt his heart
screaming to be let out. The men wore hats
with candles in glass cases at the front,
and when the lights went out he felt the air,
darker than any burial, gone dead
like air unfit for healthy men to breathe.

He heard the earth above him and the timbers
creaking, bosses barking orders ahead.
One candle lit, and he could see the walls
around him, chiseled passages and rooms.
And every whisper, every digger's step
so amplified it seemed the earth was speaking,
but in a language none could understand.
They followed rails deep in as they were told,

then deeper down—a cabled elevator
scraped its stanchions, agonies of steel
that echoed up the shaft. He heard a prayer
in Greek. The elevator stopped. A boss
gave him a shove. "Number 12. Wops out here."
Louis translated for the other Greeks,
all except the man's mistaking who
they were, and by default he led his crew

into a moaning chamber full of coal.
That day they trundled blasted rock above
from Number 12 to load in larger cars
on rails so mules could haul
the tonnage out to men who kept the scales.
The work in Number 12 made Louis scream
inside, but like the other men who worked
shoulder to shoulder with him in the seam,

he seldom spoke, afraid to show his fear.
39 cents a ton,
and now he learned what weight men called a ton.
His wages garnisheed to cover costs
of transport, housing, all he had to buy
at the company store, he worked that day
for nothing but new calluses and sweat
and the happiness he felt when it was done.

Louis Tikas walked out of the Frederick mine,
one of the working men who saw the light
and laughed, and tried to hold themselves erect
though they were tired and hungry, and felt the weight
of all the earth no longer on their backs
as if to smother them, then saw the fence,
the guards, and out beyond, the striker's tents
where union men stood watching—out of range.

I'll stay, he thought, *until I'm making money.*
I can't go back until I've seen it through.
That night he shaved his mustache in gray water
because it had only held the dust too close,
and in the spotted mirror saw his face
would not come clean. The lifelines in his palms
were creased with black that he could not wash off.
He ate a tin of beans and went to sleep.

—∞—

Mountains. Distant sea a dream above the olives.
His sisters going out to milk the goats
while he repaired a terrace wall. The weight
of stones.
            He woke with burning hands,
the pain of blisters, in a man-packed room
dark as the chambered pit but full of snores.
The freedom of his dreams
far off as sunlight on a swirling cove.

For all the years he'd lived in America
he'd felt the torture of its emptiness.
The quiet of a village just at nightfall,
goat bells, women's voices, rustle of leaves,
came back as steadily as waves, as wind
in olive branches he had climbed as a boy
to feel them swaying like small boats at sea.
He felt that constant sway and almost cried.

Already Louis knew that he would quit,
but when and how, how many Greeks he'd take
straight to the union hall in Frederick—
those were the questions that disturbed his sleep.
How they would leave. How pass the guarded gate.
He'd seen detectives in a motorcar,
armed men from Baldwin-Felts,
the agency well known for breaking strikes.

And so he rose and worked, went down the pit
and learned to push his fear still deeper down.
The men who argued at the scales were beaten
senseless by the guards while Tikas watched,
but each night after work the Greeks would talk
of *apergíes*, strikes, and what it meant
to be a scab, and how long they would wait
and what some unarmed men could do to guards.

Now men brought news about the Balkan war,
while others talked of Democrats elected
here in America: Woodrow Wilson,
the landslide President whose coattails swept
Elias Ammons, Colorado's new
and sympathetic governor, to office.
Outside the wire men had another life.
"Our task," said Tikas, "is to get outside."

—⚍—

"So who's the little Wop out front?" the Pit-boss
asked the man from Baldwin-Felts. Midday,
November 17th. Louis had dropped
his pick. "*Eláte, paidiá. Páme!*"
Come, boys. We're going! Now he stood
with sixty Greeks—too many for the guards
to shoot—and said, "You gonna open gate?
We got a right to go. You can't stop us."

The Baldwin-Felts man and the Pit-boss stood
a hundred yards away, and watched the gate
swing open. "Tikas," the detective said.
"Some pain in the ass. Maybe a union plant."
The Pit-boss shook his head. "That little runt
has wrecked our total for the day and riled
the men below. You keep an eye on him,
and while you're at it, send me some more guns."

—⚍—

The shantytown of Frederick had a hall,
a clapboard building where the men on strike
lined up each week to get their union pay.
These men were shouting when the throng of Greeks
marched to the head of the line.
Some little guy named Tikas, ram-rod straight
in sweater and work boots like he owned the joint,
said, "I bring to the union sixty-three Greeks!"

Two days later the entire working force
of the Frederick mine walked out in one block.
The boys from Baldwin-Felts were mad, broke up
a meeting claiming Tikas had a gun,
but he slipped out before they could arrest him.
Two months later, in a boarding house
in Lafayette, Tikas dove from the back door
ahead of detectives shooting guns at him

while Greeks shouted, "Run like the hell, Louis!"
He felt a bullet bite the flesh above
his right elbow, but kept on running fast
around a stable and away from lights
into a darkness that protected him.
About this time John Lawson down in Denver
heard of the Greek who could speak English well
and keep his head whenever bullets flew

and said, "Now you go out, you find that boy.
You patch him up, buy him a suit and tie
and bring him here—he's in the union's employ,
okay? Three-fifty for a working day
and all he's got to do is follow me."
So Lawson's word went out. Tikas was hired.
He gave up digging coal and selling coffee,
though he stopped by the shop to be admired.

"A new man." Gus and the Scholar touched his coat.
"The union's got you now, my boy. Watch out."

7. *Meeting Mother*

"That girl," said Mrs. Reed. "You send her on
a simple chore and find her hours later,
dreaming down by the river." She and Pud
stood in the August heat outside the house
on Prospect Street. Pud had a stick and drew
arroyos for the ants to cross in a spot
where grass would never grow, while Mrs. Reed
pinned laundered sheets to a line and gossiped

across the yard to Mrs. Kane next door.
Pud saw the women's heads bobbing above
the lapping white like waves blown on the river.
Nearly three, he loved to watch the ants.
Once he took a stick to a red ant hill
and made them mad. They climbed inside his pants
and bit him up and down until he bawled.
Luisa split a yucca leaf for salve.

Now he ruled a little road of ants,
set up twig fences, made them get around
or bridge them. Nothing stopped them getting back
to their sandy mound at the yard's far edge.
He heard his mother talk about Luisa,
gone two hours. Her voice on white waves. The sun
gave her a squint and made her face go pointy
when she tied her hair back in her kerchief.

Then Mrs. Kane would talk across the breeze—
how Daisy and the other girls were better.
"The other day I went out to the shed
for a bucket of coal, and Daisy left her game
and come right over and lugged it for me
like I was too delicate to work." Pud saw
how big the belly was on Mrs. Kane,
who stooped with difficulty at her basket.

"That's how you come to be," his sisters had told him.
"Mama's belly was big as that—so big
she had to lie abed for months and months.
And that was when Luisa came." Pud loved
Luisa, loved to get in close and smell her
though Daisy said she had a Mexican smell.
He loved to sit between her legs, lean back
against her chest and feel her arms surround him.

He listened when she told of mining camps
where everybody had a funny name
and blew things up, or so it seemed. Or how
the ghosts came floating down the canyon roads
for a day of the dead, came out of mines
and visited the houses where they lived.
How ghosts were never scary, only sad
because they couldn't touch the ones they loved.

Now his mother talked about his sisters
who were playing up the street, what each one
said or did that made her laugh aloud.
Luisa only seemed to get more clumsy,
her long legs disconnected from her brain,
so once she tripped as she came up the steps
and chipped a tooth, which was too bad because
she was nearly beautiful.

"You'll have to watch that one," said Mrs. Kane,
and something about the boys who came sniffing.
Pud wondered if they smelled the Mexican
from down the street, the smell that drew him on,
and even now, manipulating ants,
he let his mind fall back where it was soft
the way he did at story time. He felt
her downy arms come close around his body.

He hated when Luisa left the yard.

—∞—

For her part, at fifteen Luisa felt
no part of any family, the Reeds
or even the fading memories she had
of John Mole with his corn cob pipe, or Conchata
who died so suddenly one autumn morning.
She had walked up to the store on Main Street,
George Reed and Co.—another mercantile
but independent of the company.

She never hurried on these errands, glad
to get away from girls who seemed each year
a little more resentful of her presence.
And it was Saturday. The town was full
of cars and wagons, folk who came on foot
to load up on supplies. George Reed and Co.
was bustling, cheaper than the company store
but turning a healthy profit all the same.

While Arthur wrote up orders, Mr. Reed
brought goods up for his customers. The heat
had made him take his coat off, so he worked
without a collar on, his sleeves rolled up,
and when he saw Luisa at the door
in her blue dress with the bodice she had sewn
herself, he winked and called her Sugarpie,
told her to scale the ladder, hand up cans.

And so Luisa worked two hours above
the brothers' heads, and as she handed up
big tins of beans and carrots, Mr. Reed
was there behind the counter like a god,
his perfect hair, blue eyes and blond mustache,
and the way he laughed and seemed to know the name
of every customer who came, furtive
or well-to-do. They called him Mr. Reed

and praised the thriving shop. When they wanted guns
he unlocked the case, held the polished barrels
away from people, talked of ammunition.
He'd spin the chambers of a Colt six-gun,
take aim at the stuffed elk head that hung
on the far wall over the boots and shoes
and tell how he had shot a rattlesnake
with such a pistol. Then he'd wink her way—

Luisa's knees would weaken on the ladder
so she held a rung to keep from falling off.
Arthur Reed was younger, stronger, but he
never had the same effect as George did.
Something about the married man, the voice
when George Reed spoke, especially to women.
He seemed to own the world, a world so far
from mundane Prospect Street.

Late for the midday meal, Luisa left
with a gunny sack of stuff for Mrs. Reed,
sweets for the kiddies, and at the shop door
heard some stranger saying, "*La huerfana,*"
and turned to look at eyes that turned away.
Someone from the camps. Someone who had known
her story or had seen her when she left?
She almost stayed to talk.

"*Mas vale algo que nada,*" said a voice.
Half a loaf is better than none. And she
could see they had gone on to something else.
And then the door shut with its jingling bells
and she was in the heat and crowd, turning
down Commercial Street and toward the river.
There on another day she might have waded
to cool her feet, but she knew Mrs. Reed.

It wasn't temper—just exasperation—
the sheer effort of getting a thing done
like dinner with four girls and a small boy
dashing about the house. Luisa felt
so slow and absent-minded as she helped,
as if her helping only made it harder,
her mind on George Reed and his blond mustache,
the way he winked and called her Sugarpie. . . .

—⚹—

After she put Pud down at his bedtime
Luisa sat on the steps to the front porch
to catch the evening breeze.
The girls were playing jump-rope in the yard
and Mrs. Reed, her mending basket out,
rocked and looked at the view of Fisher's Peak.
The men worked late a summer Saturday.
Luisa gazed across at town, the river.

That was where they came from—pistol shots
in quick succession: POP-POP-POP. POP-POP.
A ricochet of sound from buildings where
Commercial Street fanned out above the river.
"What in tarnation?" Mrs. Reed had stood.
POP-POP. POP-POP. POP-POP. Luisa ran
almost before she knew it—wind rushing
past her ears, black hair flying. Behind her

voices screamed, "Luisa, no!" But no one
followed as she crossed the thumping bridge,
more people near, then running too like her,
both men and women. Then they were a crowd
and she stopped running. Motorcars and people
jammed the street outside the union office.
She saw the smashed glass of a shop window,
the bullet holes and chips in the brick walls.

A man lay on the pavement, holding his knee
and cursing like a soldier. Another man
lay twisted on a thick stream of his blood.
Some women screamed. Policemen cleared a way
to get an ambulance to the wounded man.
Luisa stood, relieved it wasn't George.
No, it was George Reed standing next to her:
"What the hell are you doing here, young lady?"

He'd put his collar on, his coat and tie
with its cigar smells. Sometimes, walking home,
he liked to smoke, and maybe stop to drink
just one with Arthur before he crossed the bridge.
She felt him turn her from the sight and walk
deliberately away, his hand upon
her shoulder, steadying her shaking bones.
"Who was that man?" she asked. "The one who died."

"Some union fella, came in on the train.
I heard him having words with two mine guards
or detectives or whatever the hell they are."
He stopped and turned her toward him, and she saw
worry in his blue eyes. "It's getting worse,
young lady. More union men arriving
every week, and more detectives. These fellas
argued. I didn't see who started shooting.

He got lucky and hit one in the leg
but they got him four or five times. God knows
how many bullets went astray—you hear?
If you had been down here you could have been
hit yourself, and Mrs. Reed and I
would not like that." He held her by both shoulders
almost to shake her, or to hold himself.
"I never want to see you near this kind

of trouble, hear? You stay away from bullets."

—⚹—

Men talked. Men settled things. Luisa worked
and listened—in the house or at the store.
"Fella they killed was Gerald Lippiatt.
Eye-talian, so they say. Now all the Wops
will vow revenge, the way they do it there
in Italy. Honor killings. Saving face.
Those Baldwin-Felts boys better watch their backs."
Luisa gripped her broom and looked away.

Some days it seemed whole hours would pass without
the fear of gunfire, overhearing words
about the shooting and the coming trouble.
Luisa stepped into the indoor bathroom
with its mirror, saw the dark-eyed girl who looked,
the flawed smile, touched the hair that framed her face
as if a stranger touched her from a world
she never knew, and that was how the world

went on, itself, both near and far away,
where men she could not have known were talking,
the big-eared governor, his gentle face
perplexed by all this labor disagreement,
saying, "I don't see why those gentlemen
who own the mines won't recognize a union,
or why those union boys won't put away
their guns and talk. I didn't ask for this.

I came into this office with good will
toward men. I'm a man who worked my way
from childhood on. I used to melt the solder
off tin cans to sell it"—at which his staff
around the meeting table rolled their eyes.
They'd heard this one before. His sympathy
was big enough to blanket all the poor
but he was weak, they said behind his back.

He thought the hardest part of governing
was done with the election. He resisted
calling out the Guard, though General Chase
was champing at the bit
to show what week-end soldier-boys could do
to keep the peace and quell the foreign rabble.
Then there was the Bureau Chief of Labor,
the able Mr. Stewart, Ethelbert,

who warned the governor that Trinidad
required tending to for the blood that spilled,
the dramaturgy of a labor meeting:
"They're bringing Mother Jones, the socialist
Frank Hayes, the best they've got. West Virginia
whetted their hunger for another fight.
Know what Mother told the *New York Times?*
She's not for violence—she's for drama!"

"Why now?" The governor smoothed back his hair
and stood and sat and stood again. "Why us?
We're Democrats. We've proved we're on their side.
Why not give us time to make things better?
Don't they see we're friends?"
                                          And Mr. Stewart:
"They've talked their heads off. No one ever listened.
I'll go back east. Reason with Rockefeller
Junior, appeal to his better nature now—

it's our last chance to try a dose of truth."

—∭—

And pigeons at the window take the air
like a shellburst, sail above busy streets
in unison as if they were a mind
too anxious, too intense for any rest.
But out beyond the city, stillness reigns
or seems to reign in uplifted granite slabs,
in shivering aspen groves, fallen scree
and creeks that cannot whisper *Summer's gone.*

There is a voiceless beauty we adore
because we think it innocent and pure.
We call it Nature, praise its quiet soul
and save vast tracts from new development.
But Nature's haunted too, though we don't know
the names it would be called by,
the gods it would prefer we reverenced.
There is no purity. Not in this world.

There is living and there is dying. There is
far away and close. There are degrees
of sound, from coughing engines in a street
to whispers in a lover's ear, to whisks
of leaf-fall and the frozen stars beyond
our ordinary hearing. There are stories
like the one I tell you now, the teller's gaze
afloat in time and space, a camera lens

discovering September in the town
of Trinidad, bustling, bothered as a flock
of birds unsettled by buckshot. The year
is 1913. Lefty Calabrini
has stepped onto the platform from the train
and asked directions to the opera house.
He has a bulldog walk, suspicious, proud,
and wears the ribbon of a delegate.

Rounding a corner in the crowded street
he sees a young girl, maybe ten years old
with blonde hair—but it's not her he stares at
for a second time. It's the older one,
fifteen or so, and even in her dress
she has, he sees, a body he has dreamed of,
an awkward sway, a way of feeling pleasure
she's half afraid to feel.

He stops and almost laughs—Conchata Mole.
The daughter—what's her name?—is growing up.
And when the girls have seen him, the young one
staring at his mangled hand, the elder
brightening in recognition, he can't
hold laughter back. "Now there's a face I know.
It's Lefty, kid. I knew your Mom and Dad.
You're all grown up—a looker

if you don't mind a fella saying so.
A looker like your Mom.
I always gave your Dad respect, you know?
I always told him, John, you got good taste
in women. Now look at you. And who's this
little girl?"
                 "This is Daisy Reed. She's from
the family in town that took me in."
"I'm not so little," Daisy says.
                              "Well then,"

says Lefty, "maybe you can point the way."

—ɷ—

"You did *what*?" George Reed had heard his daughter
as she almost danced around the parlor
talking of the man with the mangled hand
and how they went into the theater
where crowds of men were making speeches, then
the old lady strutted across the stage
and every man went *sshh!* to listen to her
except when they were laughing their heads off.

Luisa, in the kitchen, almost froze,
hearing the anxious Reeds in the next room,
hearing her own name as the one who knew
the mangled man who took them to the show.
And afterwards, when Lefty had to speak
about complaints the miners handed him,
he seemed to growl them like an animal,
and Daisy said that they were late for dinner,

her Daddy would be mad, and tugged away
at Luisa's arm, and now Luisa fumbled
a chicken carcass at the sink, and tried
to keep track of the pot of boiling spuds
and the parlor talk, so certain she was caught
for doing something terrible—George Reed
would want to belt her for it as he had
two years ago for something—what was it—?

Beyond the agitation of the Reeds
she heard the lady they called Mother Jones
like someone's Irish Granny, though she cursed
and said that cursing was a poor man's prayer.
This is America, my friends. No Dagos,
none of the names they call you at the mine.
Once they let you in, you are American.
Fear is the greatest foe you've got. Don't fear!

Liberty is not dead—she's only resting
and it's time for us to wake her up, my boys.
I don't fear anybody. I'm going to tell
the governor of Colorado. I'm going
to stay right here and by God we will win.
If you boys are too cowardly to fight
there's women enough to come and beat the hell
out of you, so strike, boys, and stay with it!

But such applause and cheering that she caused
were doused as George Reed paced his family kitchen,
raising an arm as if to smite the air
and turning to Luisa—"Damn it, girl.
Don't you know? Didn't I tell you not to—
Did I save you from an orphanage to have you
taking my own flesh and blood to meetings?
That Mother Jones is nutty as a fruitcake!"

Luisa heard from far away, as if
an ice age had moved in from western peaks
along the Purgatoire, as if her mind
flew backwards like a frightened bird and found
the slag and filth of childhood and her skin
rebelled and stood its ground and would not hear.
He was so handsome with his blond mustache
but now she was afraid she hated him.

Then Mrs. Reed, who had a headache, said,
"George, for heaven's sake, let the girl alone.
Nobody's hurt. Nobody came back dead
and it's a legal meeting. Mother Jones
just likes to hog the limelight now and then.
It's speeches, George. It's only politics,
the way the world is going. Remember when
you talked about the company's bag of tricks?

You used to sound like one of the union men."
Her voice could calm her husband like the night
that quiets houses. With his anger gone
George Reed turned to his children. All the fright
hung in the air, though. Later, in her bed
Luisa thought of Lefty's news—how Cash
was a mine guard, while Too Tall MacIntosh
stooped in the dark to earn his daily bread.

8. *The Language of the Gun*

Tikas had seen the village of Segundo
west of Trinidad above the river,
its view of the snow-tipped Sangre de Cristo Mountains
sharp as a far-off picket of the gods.
That was where a band of his fellow Greeks
ambushed the mine guard, Robert Lee, and shot
him in the throat with buckshot. He bled to death
beside his cocked and loaded Winchester.

And Louis saw the corpse
of Gerald Lippiatt the night they came
to Trinidad, and knew the fight had started.
His job at first was to restrain the Greeks
who listened to him with untrusting eyes.
The killing at Segundo was bad news
of the sort he hoped to stop, but one man
could never cover every trouble spot.

He took his orders from a boss he liked,
John Lawson, tall and seasoned as a tree,
who knew the work and knew what justice was
and won men over with his measured speech.
Like Lawson he would be
ubiquitous as far as train and car
and horse and telephone would help him to
appear wherever trouble had erupted.

The strike demands were posted. First demand:
recognition of the union. Second:
a ten per cent advance on tonnage rates.
Third: an eight-hour work day for all laborers.
Fourth: pay for all narrow work and dead work.
Fifth: weight men elected by the miners.
Sixth: the right to choose the stores we trade in.
Seventh: enforcement of laws, and no more guards.

He'd heard what Mother Jones and wild Frank Hayes
had said of these demands—that they made sense.
He'd seen John Lawson nod his weathered head,
declaring steadily the first demand
was the one that John D. Junior would resist.
"A difference of philosophy," said Lawson
to a trusted few. "He thinks philosophy
can win against our hunger and our grief."

This in the union office on the day
nine thousand miners dropped their tools and struck.
And Louis listened with a racing pulse,
the sense of danger close.
"I'll meet you boys at Ludlow," Lawson said,
shaking his organizers' hands. "The tents
will come from West Virginia. We'll set up
the big encampment by the railroad tracks.

You men bring up your crews and families.
Tikas, you organize your people, hear?
Get them to hide their guns, come peacefully
and be prepared to wait.
That's the hard part for us now—the waiting.
and when they bring the scabs, don't beat them up,
but talk some sense to them. You understand?
Our job's to stay the course and keep the peace."

And Louis left the meeting in his suit
and tie, a full head taller in his mind
for having found both pay and purpose here
in Trinidad. He met a band of Greeks,
telling them when to gather for the hike
north to Ludlow, promising them good shelter
and the weekly union pay.
"Think of Mother Jones," he told compatriots.

"If she can show such courage, so can we."

—m—

Lawson drove the union Model T,
black and rattling like a heap of tin cans,
over the rutted road, past dusty scrub
and lines of people hefting their possessions.
Some stopped at Forbes beneath the closing mines
where Lawson ordered men to set up shelters
any way they could. By the time he drove
across the rusty railroad tracks at Ludlow

everyone he saw was soaked to the skin.
A storm had blown in from the west and north,
snuffing the sunlight, turning rain to sleet.
At the open ground where he had planned the camp
five hundred miners and their families
hunkered in the mud, surrounded by their luggage,
trying to shelter under oilskin, blankets—
whatever came to hand.

"The goddamn tents," said someone at his side.
"They haven't come. There's people leaving houses
up at the mines, hundreds more still coming
and we got nothing for them."
Lawson swore and leapt from the Model T
and splashed in his boots and jacket, giving orders.
Out here in open ground, exposed to weather
and a fresh September blizzard, Lawson worked

with steady fury that made others join him,
propping the wooden platforms built for tents
to use as windbreaks, overturning pushcarts,
sending men back south to Trinidad
for wagons and supplies. And as he worked
he tried hard not to see their disappointment,
the way ideals came slumping to the mud
and fear of what they'd chosen grew with the cold.

—⚶—

Louis wore his brand new pair of puttees
bought at George Reed's mercantile on Main.
They made his suit look funny, but were good
for marching in the late September mud.
Behind him a ragged band of Greeks cursed
the close sky and soaking sleet, forged ahead
with heads bowed, their bare hands red and cold,
the high hills entirely obscured by cloud.

They stopped at Forbes and saw the immigrants
huddled and ruinous, a union man
unloading cans of kerosene for fires.
"*Gamó to*," said a Greek. "Fuck America.
"Fuck this weather. Fuck the union, the strike.
Fuck everything that fucking grandma said
about our fucking freedom. Fuck it all.
What did we come here for? For fucking ice?"

Louis called them close so they could hear him.
Bedraggled, cold, he was inclined to feel
agreement with the man's complaints. And yet
he thought of Lawson, who had gone ahead,
and told his people they should show the strength
of Greeks who fought Bulgarians in such snow.
"Think of our brothers still in Macedonia,
freezing for the fatherland.

We're strong like them. We know what suffering means.
Don't let those union people see you whimper
like women. Winter's early. When we get
to Ludlow our friend John Lawson will have tents.
He will have food and fires to warm your hands.
Show pride. Brush off the snow and follow me!"
And as he marched north Louis felt the line
of sluggish Greeks as if he tugged them after.

Some carried rucksacks. Some had rifles slung
across their shoulders. Some carried their clothes
in sodden bags. When darkness tightened in
and snow accumulated on the ground
and Ludlow's flickering lights were still ahead,
they crouched beneath a hill that blocked the wind,
pressing together like farm animals
for the little heat their tired bodies gave.

Now Louis cursed the union, cursed himself
for wearing a flimsy jacket out of pride.
Tomorrow would be better. It must be.
Nothing could be worse than taking men
out of their shelters for some promises
he only half believed.
Tomorrow, he thought, kept by cold from sleeping,
hearing the men beside him curse in Greek.

—⁓—

At the first corpse-colored light on snowy ground
the men were up and moving, stomping boots
and swinging arms to pump blood into them.
Louis thought of Gus in Denver, coffee
heating on a stove, the Scholar's warnings:
"The union's got you now, my boy. Watch out."
"*Eláte paidiá*," he said. "Let's go."
They marched past snowy rabbit brush and sage.

Now to their left the canyons cutting west
were silent, though the glow of coke ovens
bled from somewhere near the Berwind mines,
casting a pale orange light on low wet clouds.
They trudged beneath the store at Cedar Hill
and up the Ludlow street, its buildings silent,
till it seemed a moaning rose from all the mud
ahead, a rumbling mound beyond the tracks.

And it was not a hill. It was people,
a thousand of them shaking off wet snow
and breaking up their carts for kindling.
They were exposed and shivering, their eyes
as darkly disappointed as the Greeks'.
Disaster, Louis thought. *Symforá.* Chaos
of crying children, shouting men. Work crews
fumbling armloads of wood for oily fires.

John Lawson stood in woolen cap and boots
beside the Model T,
directing men to keep their spirits up,
and grimly smiled at the approaching Greeks.
"Glad you made it, Tikas. Don't look so sad.
We've had some trouble from the railroad men
refusing to transport our tents. What's wrong?
A little weather got you Cretans down?"

Wagons bearing cookstoves had arrived,
their heavy cargo moved by men to platforms
organized in rows. A little town
of rootless families were lighting fires
with stolen fuel. Lawson stooped to put an arm
around the young Greek's shoulders. "Get some soup
in your belly, something warm for your men,
and by nightfall they'll have their spirits back."

So Louis set to work and others followed.
In days the tents arrived, the weather turned,
the colony at Ludlow almost thrived
beneath the watchful eyes of Baldwin-Felts
and other guards who gathered out of range.
Work parties went in groups to ward off beatings,
and in the meeting tent John Lawson had
an upright piano moved for sing-alongs.

Twelve hundred people lived here now—largest
of the strike camps in the southern coal fields.
When ground dried the men paced out a diamond
for baseball games. Women strung laundry lines
between the tents where twenty languages
were spoken. Louis Tikas made his way,
not only speaking for the Greeks, but also
welcoming folk from every fatherland.

He was, with the Croatian, Mike Livoda,
one of the right-hand men John Lawson used
to run the camp. They set up phone lines, a tent
for courtroom, another for a hospital,
and that was where he met Pearl Jolly,
the miner's wife who said that she could nurse
and seemed to look at him with flirting eyes—
this handsome Greek in his suit and new puttees.

The mine guards mounted searchlights on high ground
and kept the strikers sleepless through the nights
by playing beams across the tents, shooting
rifles into the air and shouting curses.
Tikas had a small tent to himself,
a phone for calling Lawson in Trinidad.
Some said they saw a woman in the searchlights
dashing between the tents to be with Tikas.

Some said she wore the white dress of a nurse.

—∾—

Gunfire echoed from the hills. Out of breath,
a boy came running with the news: Mack Powell,
a striker who got work on the Greens' ranch
herding cattle, was hit by a stray bullet.
The Berwind guards were aiming for some Greeks
out stealing fire wood, and when they heard
they'd shot an unarmed, married man, they laughed
and told Powell's widow where to find his body.

A few days later Louis took his leave
to run an urgent errand up in Denver:
October 13, 1913, Tikas
raised his hand with other immigrants
and in the sight of all his Denver friends
became a citizen. Next day he marched
with Mother Jones to publicize the plight
of miners striking in the southern camps.

No time to waste. He kissed the granny's cheeks
and raced back on the train to Trinidad,
skillfully feigning innocence as guards
patrolled the aisles, eyes peeled for union men.
He met John Lawson in the union office.
"Fifty fellas just got jailed for picketing
here in town. I can't budge. You go to Forbes,
Louis, and tell me what they're up to there."

And Tikas, wanting nothing more than one
night's freedom in his solitary tent,
a brief liaison with the willing nurse,
hopped a north-bound freight and left the rails
to join men huddled in the camp at Forbes.
"They got a secret weapon," one reported.
"Steel plates on a car they call the Death Special.
They claim we shot at them, and now they aim

to mow us down first chance they get." That night
he got his broken sleep, a Yankee now
on the plank floor of a tent full of men
who snuffed their lamps and waited in the dark,
nudged each other when they could hear a car
above them on the hill.
"That's the Baldwin-Felts," a man named Ure
declared in a voice made reedy by his fear.

They woke to gunfire somewhere up the canyon,
maybe close to where they'd moved their women.
Louis looked at men who hadn't slept
and felt his spirits dampened as he had
the day he led the Greeks to Ludlow. Now
he opened a tent flap and stepped outside
and saw the strangely armored car, the guns,
and men observing across open ground.

"Careful," said Old Man Ure. "These boys is mean
and they's just looking for a reason to shoot.
They know we ain't as strong as the Ludlow camp.
They aim to break us up—one camp at a time."
Louis saw that one of the guards had left
the car and crossed the field, waving a white flag.
Impulsively he started toward the man.
"I wouldn't do that if I was you," said Ure.

But Louis kept on walking—Lawson said
they had to keep the peace and he would keep it.
The air was cool despite the early sun
and he felt strangely unafraid. The man
approaching him had strapped a gunbelt on
over an unraveling sweater, his hat
tipped back so Louis saw his narrow face,
a flag in one hand, bottle in another.

"You speak English?" said the man, who stopped
an arm's length off. "You want a drink?" He held
the bottle out and Louis, who had had
no breakfast, took it to his mouth and tasted
whiskey for the first time in all his life.
"So," said the guard. "You like that? English?"
"Yes," said Louis. "I am interpreter."
He drank again and passed the bottle back.

The guard wiped it with his flag. He too drank.
"Well, look out, son. We are liable to shoot.
You understand me?" Louis felt his blood
stand still, or seem to flow into the field,
all comprehension gone. "Excuse me, please?"
he said. "Excuse me?" And the guard: "I'd run
if I was you." He turned
and started walking back to the line of men.

Louis ran. He saw the tents ahead,
heard his own quick breaths and the whipping grass
and then the snap of bullets past his head.
Before he knew it, Old Man Ure had grabbed
his wrist and yanked him up the slope. They dove
through an open flap, and Louis curled up tight
behind a stove. Someone made a noise
and then he knew that noise was his own scream.

Bullets cut the tent. Across the field
the TAK-TAK-TAK was hardly noise enough
for all the havoc in the camp, bullets
hitting cookstoves, knocking stovepipes loose,
tossing coffee pots and china urns
in pieces everywhere. And then the screams
were coming too from other men in tents
not far away. And then the shooting stopped.

A yell went up across the field, as if
a crowd of cowboys had just joined a dance,
and distant laughter mingled with the screams
inside the tents. Louis looked at Ure
who shook his beard and seemed to mutter prayers.
"You like that?" a guard called across the field.
"You tell folks you just met the Death Special.
We'll keep at it till you boys leave the camp."

More shooting came, sporadic, just enough
to pin them down, but Louis crawled out back
beneath the canvas, snaking over mud
until he reached another tent. He heard
rain pattering on the cloth, now and then
another bullet ricocheting off
a stove or ripping fabric. Half the time
he thought of the expense to clean his suit,

but such thoughts left him when he saw the boy
named Marco with nine bullets in his legs,
and later the man named Luca, shot dead
and crumpled as if a fist had knocked him down.
All right, thought Tikas, what would Lawson do?
He'd try to keep the peace.
What peace, you idiot? There is no peace.
So this is how you become American.

—⁓—

When Louis got to Ludlow he telephoned
to Trinidad and gave a full report.
Lawson hurried north on that night's train
then went with him next morning back to Forbes.
They found their way blocked by that covered car,
but Louis stopped his boss from picking a fight—
men paused in Denver,

                          paused in Trinidad,
New York and Washington, and held their breath.

One Mr. Stewart, Ethelbert, would view
reports quite distantly—how Rockefeller
preached an "Open Shop" and saw the union
trapping miners, now geared up to fight:
If Caliban learns
his masters' language and uses it to curse him,
the blame cannot be all on Caliban,
for he has learned the language of the gun.

It was a witty summary, to be sure,
though wit means little in the face of war.

9. *Rednecks*

Two Tall cursed and stooped from the open tent flap,
seeing his Mrs. pinning laundered clothes
on a windy line. A fine October day,
the sun already scooting from the Black Hills
across the flat and open space of Ludlow.
His boys had scattered hours before he woke
despite his warning to stay close to camp.
It seemed a camp of women to him now.

They ran the place. They didn't quit their work
when husbands struck. He never meant to strike
but one day all the men around him dropped
their tools in one disgruntled clatter, and he
went with them, shared their bottle and got drunk,
and Lefty came and badgered them to join
the union. That night Too Tall met his wife
and she saw instantly what he had done.

"Ye've joined the cause. Well and good. Well and good,
ye daft man, and fou as well. They'll make us leave
and live in tents, and all the work ye've done
for nothing."
                    "Aye," he managed.
                                        "Aye," she answered.
And now he took a step like a man learning
over again some new technique for walking,
another night's bad whiskey splitting him
in two like the dull head of a broad axe.

The Mrs. scowled his way but wouldn't talk.
Twice in his life Two Tall had gotten drunk—
well, maybe more than twice, but hardly ever.
He was one of those Scots whose work and virtue
turned him into the man that others sought,
wanting advice from how to lay a charge
to splinting broken bones. Not like that Lefty
who would break his fist across a stranger's face

sooner than ask the time of day of him.
Too Tall was dignified, slow to judge
and slower still to act, so on the day
he quit the mines he was not among the first.
But he could see that staying in the shack
and watching Robles, Lefty and the others go,
his wife and sons would not be safe for long.
A man who acts alone is never safe.

124 ∾ Ludlow

So it had gone some weeks now, meeting men
who talked the strike away as best they could,
their women holding family life together.
Men who chewed or smoked tobacco, looked down
at worn boots as they listened. Some had heard
how Karl Marx had a system for the poor
and how one day the revolution would
up-end corruption that made others rich.

They talked of capital and labor. Men
like that little fellow, Tikas, translated
for the others listening with their eyes, their hands
itching to do more than wait. Two Tall saw
more sorts of people than he'd ever seen:
the Japanese who brought tomatoes from
abandoned garden plots, the wary Greeks,
the Mexicans whose wives worked their *metates*—

and all would listen when John Lawson stood,
broad shouldered in his suit, the meeting tent
jammed full of immigrants who sought good news.
Now Too Tall stood upright and slowly walked,
feeling his disapproving wife behind
his back, until he found men loitering
in and out of the big tent, and Tikas
in puttees and suit, barking broken orders.

John Lawson strode among them and the crowd
followed him inside the tent. He took
the little stage and waited for the quiet,
then spoke the bad news from New Mexico,
an explosion at the Dawson Mine down there
with hundreds buried. Wind touched the canvas
overhead and for a moment no one
stirred or shuffled, coughed or said a word.

Wheesht, said the wind, and Too Tall thought of Mole
and others who had perished in explosions,
his own brain now exploding from the hooch.
This man John Lawson had a steady voice.
"These are," he said, "our brethren, men like you
and me, who've spent their whole lives in the dark,
and no one knows how many are alive.
These are a better reason for the pick

and shovel than some black ore for a scion.
I want volunteers to board the train with me.
The union pays for any man who'll work."
And Too Tall hardly thought.
His stomach growled. His skull was splitting open,
but he had to go. A man who barely walked,
he ran now to his Mrs. at the line,
and what he felt in giving her the news

was the closest thing he knew to happiness.
"It's work," he said. "I don't know what to do
with so much idleness.
I'll not be long. But when the boys come home,
give them a task that's closer to the tents
and coury them—no knowing who's about."
And even Mrs., her ferocity
now gone, reached up and kissed his bearded cheek.

—⚉—

That was a kiss he felt for thirty years
or more. Days after she was buried
he stood at the gate before their wee house
in Pueblo, touching the skin above his whiskers
as if his fingertips were a pair of lips
and he might turn to find her there again,
calling him by his real name, calling him
Christie MacIntosh. But she was gone

and they had never made it back to Ayrshire,
never again declared a day was soft,
a Sunday not for laboring. A war
raged somewhere out of earshot, his own sons
too old for it thank God but too involved
with work and families of their own to stay
and visit an old man in a steel town.
They'd buried their Mum and gone back on the train

to Denver and L.A., and Christie walked
his hot, dry neighborhood alone each day
before his lunch. Sunglint off a windshield.
He turned—some neighbor wasting rationed gas—
and once again his fingers touched his cheek.
How soft she'd been at that good-bye. And he
had never told her all about the fash
of Dawson, how men climbed the scaur to dig

with any tool they had, the few survivors
telling of a misplaced charge, the mine's mouth
shooting flames out like a dragon, and now
the blackened bodies hauled on tarpaulins
down the stumbling slopes, the feart men stunned
to silence, body after body, some
with burnt arms reaching after death, the flesh
in charred strips stiff on the bone and sinew.

His cousins in the trenches of the Somme
would write of a smell like that, perhaps, the cries
of men and animals from No Man's Land.
He saw John Lawson had to dodge the guards
and he saw Tikas—now almost famous due
to Ludlow, but then an unknown dandy—work
around the clock, knowing many dead
were Greek, and many more from Italy.

The corbies flocked to piñon scrub observing
wagons loaded with the sooty sticks
that once were men. Two hundred sixty-three.
"Our brethren," Lawson said.
Then Ludlow—everything so hard and fast
for months. Too few remembered now. The wars
had blotted out the past. Except old men
like Christie MacIntosh who had gone to work

to feed his family after the whole turmoil,
after the killings and the failures, after
the union sold John Lawson out, after
the long disgraceful struggle came to nought.
He'd shoveled coke into the furnaces
of Pueblo's mill until they made him lead
a crew, then moved him to the office where
he tallied loads of coal until retirement.

Three decades passing like a dust bowl cloud,
a long train wailing through the arid night
freighted with lives he'd never see again.
That long train hauled the grief
mined from the mesas by the immigrants
into a silence like forgetfulness.
A gunshot? No, a neighbor's car backfired.
He touched his cheek and walked into his house.

—∽—

Back then, he would recall, you couldn't sleep
until you'd seen the last corpse carted out,
and even when he'd followed Tikas, Lawson,
and Mike Livoda back to the Ludlow camp
he couldn't sleep. October 25th,
the day men lined up for their union pay,
those who'd seen disaster down at Dawson
queued in the pall of it, hardly speaking.

At that time, Too Tall MacIntosh recalled,
he didn't know about the shootings up
in Walsenburg. The sheriff's men had tried
escorting a nervous scab's wife and her kith
past marching strikers. Stones were hurled. Then shots
zig-zagged on Seventh Street
and when the running ruck had quieted
three miners lay dead on the bloody street.

After the shootings at Forbes, the Dawson mess
where guards would beat a man who tried to help,
and after Walsenburg's King Farr had barred
himself into the courthouse, armed to the teeth,
it looked like war. Law was company law.
The tents at Ludlow rustled with the news.
The hidden guns came out.
The men tied red bandanas at their throats

so you could tell a miner from a guard.
Sometime that afternoon a call came in—
trainload of deputies heading south to Ludlow—
and Lawson ordered a band of armed Greeks
north to hold them off. The meeting tent
was transformed swiftly to a command post,
peace-loving Lawson to a general
shouting commands to small teams of men.

"Boys, pitch a tent in that dry arroyo
for the families—keep 'em low, out of sight.
Too Tall, Lefty, you come with me." They hauled
a heavy wagon to the kitchen tent,
and with no horses used themselves for strength.
By now they heard the gunshots to the north
and others to the west, sped their loading
supplies to keep them safe.

With men for mules they heaved the wagon out
beyond the tents until they had it running
on the stony ground, down the wide arroyo
where the women waited, counting children's heads
and hunkered under the ruddy lip of earth.
"All right," said Lawson, nodding, out of breath,
"first thing we do is prevent a massacre,
you understand? They'll be bringing guards in

from all directions, fast as they can run.
Our job's to pin them down, but if you have to,
kill them." He pointed southwest of the tents
to the section house where the Berwind rails
came out just beyond the town of Ludlow:
"They got a mess of guards down there. Our boys
have pinned them in the section house for now."
The tart air had filled with rapid gunfire.

"Some of Louis's Greeks went after Karl
Linderfelt," said Lefty. "That fucker thinks
he's General Pershing."

                    "You got a gun?" said Lawson.
"I know where to find one," said Lefty.

                               "Good.
Too Tall, you and Lefty lend those Greeks
a hand, let them know you got explosives
if you need to. Put your red bandanas on
and keep your heads down, this is serious."

Too Tall ran with Lefty among the tents
and found a rifle in its hiding place,
half ran, half scuttled to the steel bridge
over the Berwind road. A clutch of Greeks
lay in the shelter of the bridge's berm,
taking pot shots at the section house,
and now and then a bullet from the guards
clanged on the rails, the bridge, or sprayed gravel

over some cursing redneck's head. Lefty
looked like a man who'd never been so glad,
steadied his barrel with his mangled fist,
squinted along the sight and with his left
hand squeezed the trigger, firing at a window.
Too Tall spotted for him, saw the siding
splintered by their gunfire, the shattered glass.
He saw a deputy outside roll over,

struck by bullets, dead, and how the body
twitched each time another bullet struck it.
He saw a man he later learned to hate,
the blond guard, Karl Linderfelt, escaping
toward the Green Ranch and the wooded hillock.
Dark had fallen, but he saw their shadows
and failed to tell the other men to fire.
"I'd never been so feart," he later said,

and unlike Lefty had no heart for killing.

—⚈—

Two mine-filled canyons emptied on the flats
of Ludlow, and in that stony open land
the little banks and hillocks were too few
to stop chaotic crossfire. That weekend
bullets spat and skirled from all directions.
At night the rednecks pulled back by the tents
to guard their families, but small teams crept
up hills and canyons, men like Louis Tikas

and Mike Livoda running ammunition,
hoping the guards would not get their machine gun
close enough to fire upon the camp.
And when the Greeks burnt down the section house
they first ransacked it, found a side of beef
and other food to haul back to the tents.
At dawn one morning bullets flew among
the falling snowflakes. Home-made bombs were thrown.

West of Ludlow houses at Tabasco
shuddered, struck by bullets. A man named Wooten
got his children up—his wife refused
to run for safety, never having dreamed
that lead could splash into her dining room
like this, until she saw her daughter hit,
her small arm bleeding, then her boy struck too
in the hip, the bone shattered.

Too Tall knew Frank Wooten well enough,
a good man, a company man wanting
only what the rednecks wanted, only
the decent life America had promised.
And now Frank Wooten scuttled among rocks
to Berwind, hoping to fetch the doctor, seeing
men he used to work with
aiming their smoking rifles at his town.

"It was an ugly battle," Too Tall said
whenever he was asked to tell of it.
"Not that any battle's ever dainty."
The Wooten children lived
but there were guards and miners killed, enough
to get the mild governor's attention.
He sent in the militia to disarm
both sides, but of course within a fortnight

those Sunday soldiers understood whose side
they would be on. It was the C. F. & I.
that buttered their bread.
                              And mass hysteria
engendered by that first October battle
maddened the eyes of rednecks and their wives
and made the angry guards like Linderfelt
join the militia for a chance to kill
some immigrants with darker colored skin.

"Aye," said Too Tall. "John Lawson's one mistake—
trusting the troops to safeguard striking miners."
It wasn't the way that men who had a stake
in coal and steel, who rode in plush diners,
played golf with churchmen, smoked their fat cigars
and testified to Congress, saw the game.
They heard of shooting among railway cars,
sermoned their lessers about the sense of shame.

10. *The Photo in the Photo*

These are the facts, but facts are not the story. . . .
There was a weight, a person with a name.
That weight is gone, in ashes or in earth.
The name accrues some glory,
but just as surely dies—much like the dream
of freedom. One man's calculated worth,
the kitchen worth of women for whom work
was never-ending, fall into the dark.

The facts, the facts. I buy a battered book
about the massacre at Ludlow, and the man
who sells it to me asks a modest price,
and with a heavy look
tells me how "the whole thing got out of hand,"
the union played up tales about the vice
of lawmen, victims in the burning tents.
"It wasn't a massacre of the innocents."

And I assure him I'm not here to judge,
but fail to mention what I dream of writing:
a tale in verse about the immigrants,
the pluck me stores, the dodge
of truth among arroyos where the fighting
razed all hope of prospering, and the fenced
land hardened and the people went away
and died as surely as they lived a day.

—∭—

I have a photo of a photo pinned
on an artist's easel, around it many holes
from pins that almost look like bullet holes.
The photo in the photo's of a girl,
identity unknown, in flowered smock,
her dark hair rising from her forehead in
a crest, then bound behind her head, the rest
flung forward over her right shoulder.

She seems mestizo, pretty, with a look
that sees beyond her time, almost to ours.
I wonder whether, if she smiled, I'd see
a front tooth slightly chipped,
the slightest flaw intensifying beauty.
This is my image of Luisa now,
found in a Denver catalog of photos
that Ollie Aultman took in Trinidad—

the same man who, some three decades later,
would photograph my father and his brothers
home on leave from theaters of war.
And so I see Luisa
standing by as he tests magnesium lights,
then moving to her corner while the Reeds
are gathered for their formal portrait. George
with trimmed mustache, the worn-out beauty of

his wife, the squirming girls, the pudgy son
who can't stop staring at the other girl
outside the family portrait.
                        Later, the bath
of chemicals, and whose face should appear
but this young serving girl, part Indian
perhaps, a print no larger than a thumb.
He pins it to his easel, leaves it there
for days, and photographs the photograph.

How odd that he has done that—and a girl
who didn't pay and hardly said a word.
Photographer and subject, bound by a cord
of silence, look into each other's world.

11. *Blizzard*

The talk by firelight in the militia camps
was mostly about pay, and how the old
eye doctor, General John Chase, had worn
a peacock uniform to inspect the troops.
But the stocky, whip-smart Karl Linderfelt
could spin a yarn or two of other wars
and sing forbidden songs
like "Damn, Damn, Damn the Filipinos."

"The thing is, he began, his meaty hands
fanning sparks and woodsmoke into darkness,
"you need a man like Chase to talk some sense
to weaker men like Ammons. You need to know
when force is all you've got. I came down here,
lived with the mine guards for a week or two
to see how they progressed against the strikers."
He shook his slab face. "Half measures won't do."

Back in the uniform of the National Guard,
Linderfelt was frank to General Chase,
who took that frankness to the Governor
and L. M. Bowers, Chairman of the Board
for the C. F. & I. And so it was,
this Midwest Scandinavian who'd gone
from college drop-out to a soldier's life,
could almost will those higher up to act.

"In the Philippines," he said into the fire,
"you had to learn which niggers you could trust
and there were very few.
You went out alone, we might find you dead
with your balls sawed off. So we went in groups
and if we thought a village fed insurgents
we just burned it down. That's how we acted there.
Same thing with Madero down in Mexico—

when you've got people out of uniform
you have to wonder who you're shooting at.
That was a war I didn't like. Still is.
Those Mexicans keep killing Mexicans
like they don't give a damn. Uncivilized.
That's why so many of them want to live
up here with us—because Americans
still have respect for life.

That's what these immigrants, these Greeks like Tikas,
have to learn. We are a nation of laws
and anyone who walks in our back door
and flouts our laws has got to learn our ways.
These people come from places without laws,
you see, and that's the trouble in a fight.
They're liable to hide behind their women,
open fire the second you turn your back."

And on he went, and most men at the fire
listened to the man's experience,
but one uneasy soldier, ex-mine guard
whose uniform was stiff with starch, thought back
to men he used to work with at the mines—
Too Tall, Lefty and John Mole—
and now Cash Jackson, as penniless as ever,
felt the night's tonnage pressing on his back.

—∞—

Tikas, awake, surprised to feel such grief,
tasted the salt of tears that came in dreams
and knew what he had missed was almost freedom,
years ago in sunlight when he drank
the virgin pressing of the oil like wine
at his father's house. *Oh God*, he missed the sea,
the tears of an eternity of men,
the peacefulness of swimming under water.

He missed the smell of grass in autumn rain,
the sacks of dripping goat cheese hung from rafters,
the words like *thálassa* and *ouranós*
that felt to him much weightier than English.
Words in American were cardboard words,
cast-offs of language naming nothing real.
Something was wrong here, something very wrong
with a people who could never sing for joy.

Beside him, breathing deeply, her pale breasts
melted into his ribs but pulsing faintly,
the nurse, Pearl Jolly, who again crept in
in darkness, and who made love with a joy
he had seldom known, fidgeted in dreams,
and he could almost feel her sailing in sleep
to territories he could not imagine,
spice islands of ambition, loss and love.

He knew her being here was dangerous
and it would have to stop,
but what good was the little power he had
if women were not drawn into his tent?
And after all, the ancient Greeks would say,
our life is short and we should take such joy
because the end of life is utter dark.
And then he heard objections from the priest,

but just as he prepared apologies
Pearl started, blinked her eyes, and seemed to peel
her body off from his.
They nodded to each other—shadow puppets
in the play of searchlights over canvas walls.
A last kiss and she groped for underthings—
she'd arrived uncorseted—and swiftly closed
herself in clothes and slipped into the night.

Somewhere a barking dog, and later footsteps,
but since the militia came no pot shots
were fired above the tents by drunken guards.
It seemed a lull, like January days
in Greece—Halcyon Days—
when calm and sunny seas could make you think
the winter passed, but always storms returned,
thrashing the olive trees, roiling heaven.

So his mind went as the wet touch of a woman
grew fainter in the memory of skin.
He felt the rash of kisses on his chin
and knew that she'd be rasped and reddened too
because he had not shaved that day; the dark
and her husband's drunkenness would save her from
discovery. He touched her in his mind,
afloat in freedoms he had never known.

—⚒—

Ever since the death of Gerald Lippiatt
the Baldwin-Felts detectives lived in fear
of anarchists with guns, and went in groups
for self-protection. That September shoot-out
left George Belcher, the West Virginia dick,
with a bad leg and an even bigger chip
on his shoulder concerning striking immigrants,
and that was what he carried back to work.

He also carried certain plates of steel
strapped about his torso under his shirt
to stop assassins' bullets.
                              Someone knew
about the plates. Someone saw George Belcher
stepping off a curb in Trinidad
November 20th, 1913,
dashed up and put a bullet in his head.
"The Wops got their revenge," somebody said.

Louis got the news by telephone:
"They're sealing off the town, busting down doors
and scaring the daylights out of everyone,"
said Lawson. "Jailed some of our boys for singing
union songs in a bar. There've been some beatings,
some arrests. I'd say it won't be long
before your pal Karl Linderfelt surrounds
the camp and starts harassing all your people.

You tell that fella Verdi to watch out
and keep his Italians cool, and Mike Livoda
and the others. That tinhorn General Chase
has his excuse to start in bashing heads,
so watch yourself, you hear?"
And Louis stepped out of his tent in shirtsleeves,
casting his eyes in darkness for the path.
The searchlights, he noticed, had been turned off.

—◠◠—

For four days all was rumor, weakened sunlight,
flapping canvas and nervous baseball games.
Then, the 25th, Louis saw the soldiers
marching up the road, Linderfelt on horseback
in Pershing hat like the other officers.
South of the Ludlow camp, Louis Tikas
stepped in suit and tie on the rutted road
with Mike Livoda and a crowd of men

until the troops were close enough to talk.
He saw the thick-set Linderfelt push back
his hat and smile. "Well, if it ain't the Greek.
Tikas, right? I've seen enough of you
to know what I think."
                              Louis nodded back
and met the soldier's eyes and said, "Someday."
"Oh yeah?" said Linderfelt. "Well let her come."
And that was all the two men had to say.

"We're here to search the camp," said an officer
as if to speak into the tents. "There's been
a lawman murdered down in Trinidad
and we are authorized to look for guns."
    "We have no guns," said Tikas.
"Will you disarm the mine guards also, please?
This is peaceful camp. All is families.
Women. Children. We have nobody guns."

"Line up your people, Tikas." And with that
the ranks of soldiers split and marched ahead
in two columns until the camp was circled.
The thirteen hundred immigrants of Ludlow
shuffled into a ragged line, while men
ransacked their tents, returning with few guns
and belts of bullets. All that afternoon
officers rode their shitting horses through

the quiet camp, sending their men back in
for second looks and looking at the women
staring back with hatred in their eyes.
And when the soldiers left, Karl Linderfelt
rode close to Tikas, saying, "Let her come,"
and people said that day if eyes could burn
those two men could have burned the camp with looks
unsparing in their rage.

Under the platforms of the tents were pits
the families had dug for shelter during shootouts,
and there the crated rifles had remained
safe from prying eyes. They would need more,
and while he eyed the crowd for the white dress—
the woman he had hoped would see him act
so calm before the soldiers—he was talking
about the guns and how they must get more.

—ᴨ—

The weather turned and the unsettled sky
went dark for days, then brightened over peaks
and prairies. Cut off from Trinidad by troops,
the men at Ludlow used their telephones,
but some things they could never say for fear
of spies, and so one night
Louis and Mike Livoda and Tom Perrett
walked the scrub paths half lit by the moon.

Above them, stars appeared and disappeared.
When clouds obscured the moon they had to pause,
big Mike Livoda breathing hard, his head
reshaped by beatings from the law.
At night-time Louis almost felt at home,
recalling how he climbed the hills in Crete
to find a goat that slipped its hobble and ran,
and how the moonlit olives

stood like crones on terraces below him
and the moon itself across the sea, a path
of silver water leading to its face.
Now they used the light to look for the mesa,
Fisher's Peak, and gauge how far they'd come.
Close to the town they heard a kind of hum
and smelled the burning coal
and Perrett went ahead to scout the way.

He came back with his arms above his head,
militia rifles at his back. A rush,
and Louis turned, and there beside a road
a whole patrol ran at them, rifles aimed,
and there were lights, and Louis, thrown face-down
on gravel, felt his arms yanked behind
his back, his wrists lashed like a hobbled goat.
"Mike! Mike!" It was his own voice calling out,

and Mike Livoda grunted next to him.

—↜—

How was it in the *Erotokritos*,
the long poem that his father knew by heart?
Two birds came into someone's prison cell
and sang of liberty? Or in a song
he half-remembered now:
What use is it to live in slavery?
They roast you on the fire both night and day,
whether you are Vizier or dragoman. . . .

So Louis paced his cell
in the jammed jail of Las Animas County Court,
reciting bits of liturgy and songs.
It was a basement cell, the unglazed window
barred above his head, where sometimes he heard
footsteps and the thunder of wagon wheels.
One blanket on his cot and his woolen jacket
were all he had against increasing cold.

He almost sniffed the change of weather, light
on the bars like dusk. The walls dropped water
and his breath steamed, and the broth they served at noon
turned quickly cold.
And one night in December snow flew in,
blanketing his blanket until he woke
and watched the little streetlit flakes of silver
float into the dark above his head.

He reached, and snow lay several inches deep
on his wet blanket, spilling on the floor,
and cellmates stirred, cursing this circumstance
and cursing just to keep their faces warm.
One man had matches and would hold a flame
above for its brief life so they could glimpse
a way to shift their bunks against the wall
and move together, desperate for warmth.

No daylight came, but guards brought down a lamp
and hung it in the hall so men could see
their snow-packed windows while the muffled world
went on outside the walls.
Then that too stopped, and rumors started up
of storms and ice, enough to end the world.
O heimónas, Schneesturm and *inverno*—
words that echoed off the freezing walls.

"What was it like?" When anyone would ask
some of the old men in the later decades
they would shudder, steel themselves, and answer,
"We had it bad, we had it bad, but we
felt pity for our friends out in the camps.
I don't think Colorado ever had
a blizzard worse that that one—six foot drifts
and the winds was howling down, just howling,

so even men who used to dig for a living
got their shovels out and dug and could not dig
as fast as that snow piled over the camp."
By morning tents collapsed. The cook stoves died
and had to be re-lit
and men with shovels tunneled from the flaps
like they were underground. So Louis heard,
after his release, but while he paced the cell

Tikas only knew that he was trapped
and underground at that, and he recalled
his terror in the Frederick mine, and paced
and felt that he would die
unless he found a way to get outside.
He tried to remember songs, thought of Pearl
and how her skin had sweated to his skin
in the heat two people made when they made love.

—⚭—

There were interrogations in the town,
held in a big hotel, where Louis faced
the General in formal uniform
and white mustache, denying that he knew
a thing about the killing of George Belcher.
They let Livoda go, and Perrett, but seemed
almost to enjoy the subtle panic
emitted by a Cretan in a cage.

Some men sang union songs in jail, some read
enormous books by Hugo, Dickens, Marx.
Some shouted epithets
at jailers. No one said a word to Chase's
armed tribunal. The day they let him go,
December 16th, Louis took the train
to march again with Mother Jones in Denver.
"Keep your eye on General Chase," she said.

"The man won't rest until he's jailed me too."

12. *A Multitude of Women*

Snow stood in drifts above the tops of doorways.
In heavy coats and furry caps the men
were out with shovels. Luisa put on wool
and worked beside them till they'd dug a tunnel
out from the door and part way to the street,
the buried city like a smoking plain,
deserted now, deprived of all its life.
A winter carol's rhythm worked inside her:

God rest ye merry, gentlemen.
Let nothing ye dismay.
Remember Christ, our savior
was born on Christmas day.
But nothing was the word of peace.
Nothing would offer love.
Nothing gave the world release
from the nothing of God above.

Maybe this was the Wrath of God,
this nothing, muffled, cold.
She felt like an outsider—odd
And very, very old.

—ᴍ—

That Christmas, families in Trinidad
brought trees hauled out of the woods on sledges,
fixed candles in their little cups and sang
in churches or in snow-filled streets, in homes
beside pianos, the carols set in deserts—
star and manger, kings and winter skies.
God rest ye merry, gentlemen. Yet news
was troubling. The world might come apart.

The Czar and Kaiser rattled swords, and down
in Mexico marauding bands and armies
crossed the desert. Luisa saw the papers
after the Reeds were through with them, before
they went with shovelfuls of coal into
the basement furnace. Men were shot and men
were beaten everywhere it seemed. In cities
far away, factory windows were smashed.

God rest ye merry, gentlemen.
    Let nothing you dismay.
Remember Christ, our Savior
    was born on Christmas Day.
But nothing was the word of peace.
    Nothing would offer love.
Nothing gave the world release
    from the nothing of God above.

Why was it that the men ignored her now
or seemed to turn away, or make their talk
of politics and business louder when
she entered the parlor with their coffee pot
and, leaning at their sides, refilled their cups?
Arthur the bachelor was often at
the house on Prospect Street for lunch or dinner.
The children loved their Uncle Arthur's games.

"I'll sell you to the Indians," he'd say
and wrestle them until they screamed with laughter.
Once Luisa thought she met his eyes
and saw their hunger, saw them lower, staring.
Abruptly he got up and found his coat
and said he had to get back to the store.
And George went looking for his humidor
and said he'd go as well,

and came back after midnight, thumping in
the hallway. Luisa could hear Mrs. Reed
helping him to bed with gentle scolding.
And Mrs. Reed—now there was love, if love
had not been buried by the winter snow—
her chapped and reddened hand
one afternoon upon Luisa's shoulder:
"Child, you've worked yourself to the bone. Now rest."

God rest ye merry, Mrs. Reed.
    Let nothing you dismay.
Remember the winter turnip crop
    is picked and put away. . . .
Funny how Luisa used to tremble
even at the voice of Mr. Reed,
and now it was the woman who sat knitting
calmly through the blizzard of children's chatter.

—∿—

"She asked for it," said Arthur. "You know she did."
A January night, the dinner things
now put away, Pud and the younger girls
fast asleep in their beds upstairs, and though
Luisa seldom felt invited in
when family gathered in the parlor, there
she was, with Daisy, sharing a chair, turning
pages of an illustrated catalog.

"No," said George Reed. "It's not intelligent.
Arrest a woman, arrest a granny like her,
you've got to know the country
will oppose it. I think General Chase
will get more than he bargained for from this."
    "They're fools," said Mrs. Reed. "Men playing soldier."
And Arthur, pacing: "Don't you see. The union's
using her—using her popularity."

"But why's she popular?" said Sarah Reed.
"Because she talks straight, seems to tell the truth."
    "But that's the point," said Arthur.
"Everybody knows she's as full of lies
as the robber barons. Everybody knows
she lies about her age, she lies about
her struggles—Ireland—every bit of it."

"Who's lying?" Daisy looked up from the book,
suddenly alert, and Arthur stoked the fire.
"This Mother Jones," he said.
"She's not a stupid woman, I'll give her that."
    "Did they arrest her?" Daisy closed the book
and looked up at Luisa. "That old lady
on the stage? The one who said those swear words?"
    "Words I didn't want you to hear," said George.

And now the story came, told by grown-ups
as they heard it, news and hearsay, gossip
and the law. It was as if Mother Jones
was daring General Chase to make a cause
of her, and he announced he'd have her watched,
but she had friends among the railroad men
who let her ride the trains
and let her off outside of Trinidad.

And she slipped into town and signed the book
in one of the hotels and drew a crowd
until the soldiers came to pick her up.
At her age, whatever age she was, the troops
were rightly nervous she might die in jail,
so they imprisoned her in a hospital,
San Rafael, above the town, fed by nuns
and guarded by young men of the National Guard.

Luisa did not dare to say a word,
but thought of Lefty at the opera house,
the speeches from the stage,
that little cursing granny with her glasses
whipping up a frenzy just by talking,
applause like thunder underneath the roof.
That night she hardly slept while Mother Jones
was near, across the river, under guard.

―∞―

Sunlight and snowmelt. In the high dry air,
except in the shade of buildings, heaps of snow
diminished, sending streams down to the river.
At night a frozen starlit glaze on streets
made walking tricky. One of the neighbors slipped
and broke his ankle and was carried in
where Mrs. Reed could splint it
and send Luisa to fetch the men for help.

She wore her boots, her woolen cap and coat,
and walked with caution to the bridge, pausing
long enough to look at moving water,
dark and touched with street-and-starlight, flowing
steadily beneath her. Almost made her dizzy
watching it go on, go on to the night
beyond the town
and out beyond all life she'd ever known.

Then Commercial Street, and near the corner
where she saw the shoot-out four months ago,
a group of women stood—maybe they'd come
from a meeting and brought the talk into the street
and looked about, breath steaming, for a sign
that any lawmen were approaching. Instead
it was Luisa watching them and knowing
she was not allowed to talk with union folk.

"Luisa Mole!" The clutch of women spoke
to her and turned her way,
then one of them, dark-faced, wearing a shawl,
stepped closer in the street. "Luisa Mole."
Señora Robles? Yes, it had to be.
Instinctively Luisa moved into her arms.
"*Que hermosa muchacha. Pobrecita.*
This is the girl, *la huerfana* of Mole."

The women gathered, sweeping her aside
as if to wrap her in their shawls, and talked
in rapid fragments about the old days
and children and their memories of camps
before the strike. Even in the half-light
Luisa saw Señora Robles crying,
felt the strong hands stroking her mittened hands.
"*La huerfana,* my girl, my pretty girl,

what you done to your smile? You break a tooth?
It only make you special, *pobrecita.*"
    "She's a lovely thing," said a woman's voice.
Luisa saw red hair spilling from a cap
and heard in that voice something musical
that brought her father back.
    "Mary," Señora Robles said, "this girl,
she Welsh like you but she half Mexican,

that's the pretty part." And muffled laughter,
eyes darting to the street, voices lowered.
The one called Mary said that there were women
coming in from all the camps to march
for Mother Jones.
They'd been to a meeting, painting protest signs,
and some would meet at the union hall tomorrow
for the March through town toward the hospital.

"Not everybody march," Señora said,
"some organize, some wait and see if they
arrest us, but we going to be brave
like Mother tell us. Tomorrow in the morning
you come see, eh? Come watch the women march."
    At that the little group broke up, and with
the impact of a kiss still on her brow
Luisa made her way to Main. The shop

was locked, lights out and quiet, so she knew
to turn downhill again, the icy bricks
hard to walk upon, and find the tavern
by the river. More than once
Luisa had been here to look for George.
She knew the door's heft, the stare of men
from clouds of smoke and talk inside. But he
would waste no time when she delivered news

that Mrs. Reed commanded him to come.

—⁂—

A night of little sleep,
helping the Reeds hitch up the heavy wagon
with George and Arthur slowed by all their drink,
and seeing them off, the injured neighbor flat
in the flatbed, the dray horse going skittish
on ice but going nonetheless, then bed,
under the down that Mrs. Reed had warmed
for fear Luisa Mole might catch a cold.

But all that night, or all she didn't sleep,
she felt the touch and heard the voice and smelled
the peppery smell—Señora,
who was so good to her those years ago,
as good as Mrs. Reed though she was poor,
who guarded her, made her eat at mealtime,
who bossed the other women in the camp
and might, tomorrow, march for Mother Jones.

—⚌—

The moment her morning chores were done, Luisa,
as furtive as could be in winter clothes,
skulked from the house on Prospect Street and ran
in sunglow to the river and across.
A crowd had gathered now
with signs and flags, filling the lower street
and oozing into alleys. Some estimates
would later put them at a thousand strong.

Already they were singing union songs
in ragged choruses, milling about
the way a crowd is many things and one,
a sort of double millipede in coats,
one end of which was largely unaware
just what the other end was doing. Luisa
tried to find Señora in the mass,
and as she pushed in she was taken in,

absorbed by energies beyond her own.
So many faces. Some of them she knew
but others she was meeting now. They laughed
with all the quick bravado of a crowd,
safe in their numbers, confident and strong.
And on the sidewalks citizens had gathered
as if to watch a festival parade.
When someone shouted, they began to move.

Some in the crowd were dressed in Sunday clothes
with feathered hats, and there were men and boys
mixing among the women, men and boys
watching from the roof of the White Front Bar.
Some of the signs said GOD BLESS MOTHER JONES,
others taunted the sheriff's men and soldiers.
Some women carried babies, some had children
dogging their footsteps. They became a column

marching together up Commercial Street.
Luisa saw a sign with MOTHER JONES
HAS NOT DONE ANYTHING THAT WE WOULD NOT DO
painted in bright letters, and holding it
Señora Robles, shouting of *libertad*.
Luisa joined her and the women sang,
and they could see ahead
small groups of mounted men were watching them.

At Main they turned north, and on the corner
Luisa saw George Reed with his cigar,
and saw too that he had seen her marching,
saw him, angry, shake his head and tug
thoughtfully on the smoke, and then her eyes
turned north the way her feet were marching
and the sound came over her,
sound of a crowd awakening to the scene

as if one mind had many parts; slowly
each part let the other know what it knew,
that mounted soldiers waited up the street
in khaki tunics, Pershing hats, with swords
at one leg, pistols at the other. There
in front of all his soldiers
rode General Chase himself, upright, indignant.
His cheeks were red above his white mustache.

He seemed to pace on horseback, back and forth,
his men behind him and a gathering crowd
climbing the Post Office steps and watching.
The women watched, and for a moment one
could hear shod hooves on brick, the snorting horses,
and the smoking town seemed to hold its breath.
"Ladies," shouted General Chase. And, "Ladies,
I must insist you halt this masquerade."

And "Ladies," he said again. "I'm in charge
by order of Governor Ammons. I am here
to keep the peace. Do not try my patience.
Turn back, or we will have to make arrests!"
The crowd-mind listened, paused,
then someone shouted, "*Lay*-dees!" and the crowd
was loud in laughter and the General blushed.
"Keep going for Mother Jones," someone said.

And on they went. Luisa saw the horse
of General Chase close up, and went to touch it
thinking only that it looked afraid, and
saw the General staring down at her
as if she were the one who'd shouted back,
and heard him blustering, "Don't pass. Don't pass."
His sword drawn, he was shouting now, "Get back!"
and seemed to swing at her,

but that was crazy—why would anyone
draw swords in Trinidad?—yes, it flashed
in air above her and his mustache flared with rage,
his horse reared—someone screamed—and down went Chase,
rattling flat and cursing on the bricks.
Luisa lowered her shielding arms, and felt
the crowd-mind turn in wonder at this sight.
The General was down!

Then up—he stood, swiping his hat from the street,
and shouted—did he really?—"Ride them down.
Ride down the women. Make them get back."
Did he though? Did she hear it? She would ask
these questions later on in jail. But now
she saw him mount and wheel his horse, and saw
the strangest sight of all—a cavalry charge
in downtown Trinidad,

men swinging the flats of their swords at signs,
at women's hats, at air above their heads,
the crowd-mind shifting from a laugh to fear
and people scattering down Main. Luisa
felt Señora take her hand. They ran
but seemed to butt into a horse's flank
and felt the soldiers' arms man-handle them
and found themselves beside the wrecked parade

bound up with all the other prisoners.

—‹W›—

In one of Shakespeare's plays the jailed king said,
"I have been studying how I might compare
this prison where I live unto the world."
Luisa studied too, the voices of
her new-found friends packing the county cells.
The one called Mary with her long red hair
had both her children with her, and when her husband
came to visit, the lovers spoke in Welsh.

When Mary sang an aria, the jail
fell quiet and the very streets moved close
and the stone walls leaned to hear. Then she sang
"The Union Forever," a song others knew
and joined in singing. Luisa sat alone,
hearing this high clear voice, this heaven-made
pure spirit—something she had never known,
and thought that she could die for such a singer.

13. *The Rising*

Some in the union office never liked the Greek,
withheld supplies from Ludlow, bluntly made their point
which was no point at all, only growing hatred
deep in union ranks for everyone who rose
without their say-so. Louis the Greek was popular.
Louis was a swell, too dandified in his wool suit
and leggings—ladies' man, part of that band of Greeks
you couldn't trust, and what if he had talked in jail?

Rumors and more rumors. Another storm blew in
and flattened tents, and Louis telephoned for coal
and one of the Irish cronies told him to go to hell.
When Louis hung the mouthpiece on its hook he felt
a subtle numbness setting in. Though he would show
no fear, he knew the fear that rivered in his blood.
The night the troops arrested women in Trinidad
it was all he could do to keep Greek snipers calm,

forestall another battle, this time on the streets,
and give some credibility to union orders.
On his side, General Chase was fuming too, a fool
whose story made the nation's headlines everywhere—
ATTACKING UNARMED WOMEN ON A PEACEFUL MARCH—
and worst of all, unseated from his rearing horse
because he'd tried to swing his sword at a teenage girl.
Oh yes, there could have been a fight. There could have been

Armageddon on the Purgatory River,
roof-top shooters, ricochets, bystanders toppled,
women dead in heaps as far as you could see,
and who prevented havoc?
When syndicates wired lies to journalists and claimed
a list of casualties from General Chase's charge,
when Chase's men proclaimed that bullets had been fired,
who kept his head? Who tried to help? Who calmed the camp?

And now the bastards wouldn't even send some coal
for their own people, all because the Greek was hated,
all because of lingering mistrust. John Lawson
left for hearings up in Denver. And that was when
the toughs moved in to muscle Louis from his post
as leader of Ludlow camp, made him leave his tent
and move in with his fellow Greeks, and made it hard,
if not impossible, for Pearl to pay her visits.

Now his nights were spent among the midnight snorers,
cursing men who slept with rifles in their beds.
His days went slack. No information came his way.
He wrote a protest letter to the union office,
had his grammar checked by Mr. MacIntosh,
sent it to Trinidad and Denver, telling how
he labored in the Frederick mines, he organized,
he took a bullet for the cause, he gave his blood,

he never sought publicity, and union men
denied what he was due. He was a personal friend
of Mother Jones, he dodged Death Special bullets
and saw the dead and wounded, he daily risked his life,
he tried to help at Dawson, tried to help at Ludlow
during the October battle, saved some lives,
organized the Greeks who could not be organized,
became American and served and served and served.

And what do they say? Time to move. Time to get out,
Louis, you've done your bit and it's not good enough.
Not good enough! Incompetent? Too pacifist?
Not eager enough to kill—is that what they were saying?
Days spent fuming, close to tears he'd never show.
No power now. No purpose. He could only wait
as he saw other men who waited, ordinary,
taking to the bottle when the bottle came around.

This was America. America was shame,
corruption, ruthless struggle, men who only cared
for power. No cause could lift its people very long,
their flags expedient,
their faith a way of shutting other people out,
their unions nothing more than gangs collecting dues,
and over everything the hypocritical rich
collecting art and smothering the immigrants.

And so it was that Louis Tikas had no task
the day the women came back to the Ludlow camp,
those who had been jailed, came back exalted by
their time behind bars, proud of their march for Mother.
He saw the wagons come, the crowds that welcomed them,
among them the teenage girl they called *La huerfana*
who had been orphaned yet again, the women said,
by marching for the cause. Someone objected. Someone

pushed her out to live among the rejected ones.

—⁂—

Lieutenant Linderfelt rode by to rub it in,
accompanied by troops for a routine inspection,
having to ask where Louis the Greek was living now.
Greeks inside their tents had shotguns ready to fire
but Linderfelt did not dismount, did not come in.
A sort of meaty centaur, he merely found the Greek
who said one word—"Someday"—and Linderfelt replied,
"Let her come," turned his horse and led his column off.

Louis watched it in his mind, again, again,
the shitting horse, the butt-end of a cigarette
tossed aside, and Linderfelt with his well armed men
trotting toward the rail bed, then down the Ludlow road.
He saw the scene when he had gone to Denver for
the hearings in which he was not called to testify,
again when congressional hearings moved down south
to Trinidad, then Walsenburg and back to Denver.

Battles, jailings, beatings were detailed before
officials, Louis heard his name but was not called
as if he were a dead man or invisible.
One day in Denver Lawson sought him out to say,
"It's politics. Nothing personal. There's too much
going on for one man to be everywhere
and I lost track of things. I'm sorry, Louis. I know
you put your heart in this like almost no one else."

But Louis saw the horse's ass, the gloating soldier. . . .

—⁂—

The man who couldn't testify came back to the camp
in the muck of March, a haggard place, all spirits low
because the nearby camp at Forbes had been dismantled
forcibly by troops, and factions opened up
at Ludlow deep enough to nearly kill the strike,
and news came of a committee back in Washington
where Rockefeller Junior went to testify
and, unlike Tikas, had the chance to have his say.

A capital the immigrant had never seen—
hell, as of this writing, a capital I myself
have never seen, though I have twenty years on Tikas,
not to mention opportunities galore—
my country's capital, its malls and monuments,
crack houses, embassies, "corridors of power". . . .
Almost ethereal, the way I picture it,
almost a principle where people happen to reside.

And that was where the gentle son of Standard Oil
held forth before respectful listeners about
his one "great principle," his cause,
abstract though it might be, that men be free to choose
to work and not give in to ideas from outside.
He did not know, of course, the details of the strike,
but left such regimens to men like L.M. Bowers,
and well-named Jesse Welborn, who as president

of Colorado Fuel & Iron, the company in question,
bore much of the strife and terror of late events,
and so the son of Standard Oil
would give his fellow patriots to understand
that there existed men who were quite prepared to say
the company would see this bit of trouble through
by giving its employees freedom to choose work
above corruption, anti-Christian sentiments,

the rule of rabble-rousing souls who levied fees
and offered in exchange
nothing but despair and lassitude and lack of faith.
And that same afternoon in far-off Trinidad
the ill-paid companies of the National Guard
reformed, their reinforcements made of former guards
and mercenaries. Karl Linderfelt would take command
of Company B at Ludlow—all he could have wished.

—⁊⁊⁊—

Legends of Tikas: a train car spilled Bulgarian scabs
at Ludlow, and the Greek, who might have sought revenge
for fallen comrades in the Balkan War, instead
went out to meet the men, explain the strike to them
and talk them into joining. Once a scab himself,
he understood how these strange things befell good men,
how loyalties were frayed. Because he fasted now
and ate no meat, he sympathized with any hunger.

Another load of scabs—these men were black, and Greeks
ran shouting "*Mávri, mávri,*" as if the devil had come,
and some of the blacks were beaten,
but here too Tikas stopped the fights, so legend says,
declaring that even Niggers (the word he used) were men
and should be given the respect due every man.
Though powerless and jobless for a time, Tikas
was everywhere. Tikas nursing the sick, a minister

without portfolio among the tested poor,
visiting a beaten Kostas Markos on his deathbed
in Walsenburg and interpreting for this man
as he gave testimony. Tikas as little guy,
the sort of fellow Charlie Chaplin might have played,
heroic, but by accident.
Tikas staying celibate for Lent, or because
Pearl Jolly thought she'd better play a saintly part

with all eyes in the camp, it seemed, on their behavior.
Tikas shaking hands. Tikas finding barbed wire
packed in a Ludlow well by men of Linderfelt
who strategized new methods of discouragement.
Tikas on his knees in prayer,
remembering the fierce priests of his childhood home
and taking in their strength from over the windswept sea
like Christ in icons coming with a burning sword.

Tikas in visionary hunger. How the Greeks
went out to scour the countryside and then returned
with a bleating lamb, and answered no one's inquiries
about the owner and the price, and grinned like thieves
who'd stolen from a Pasha in the recent wars.
The fattened lamb was kept in camp
until the men had seen the bier of Christ at Pueblo
carried on Good Friday, April 17th.

And then that Holy Saturday its throat was slit,
its blood spilled on the ground, its wool and hide scraped off
with knives, entrails boiled for soup to break the fast.
Men sang the liturgy—how death was trampled down—
and then at midnight they refrained from shooting guns
for fear of calling the militia in, but wept
and shouted, "Christ is risen!" and "Truly He is risen!"
Embraced each other. Shared the entrails of the lamb.

On Sunday the spitted meat was turned above the coals
and Greeks announced that Christ was risen. And that day
women played a game of baseball, while the men
cheered and hooted, drank from heavy barrels of beer.
Louis donned his Cretan cap, his boots and breeches.
Greeks from Peloponnesos, Greeks from Roumeli,
some in costume, some in common working clothes,
danced to *lyra* and *bouzouki*, circling the fire,

while not so far away the men of Company B
took up positions on high ground. Binoculars
surveyed the tents, the baseball field where women played.
Soldiers smelled the cooking flesh,
relaxed their gaze over barrels of machine guns,
shouldered rifles, thinking this a day of peace.
But some of the troops went down and tried to stop the game
and failed, promising tomorrow they would end the party.

—ᴧᴧ—

Music played in the big tent well into the night,
but Louis, who had had his slice of lamb, his bit
of well cooked brain, sensed that he should stay vigilant.
No one had named him leader of the camp again,
yet Lawson phoned from Trinidad
to let him know that groups of soldiers had gone north.
The leaders of the Ludlow camp, alerted, watched
for signs of trouble, taking turns patrolling the land.

Louis stood in shadows close to the lamplit tent,
its dusty floorboards thumping with the many dances.
He could smell the beer and felt himself light-headed,
tense and newly worried all at once. Inside
he'd seen Pearl Jolly, knew that she saw him as well.
He saw her clapping with the crowd, knew her body
even from a distance by the way she moved,
her husband near and sober so the way she looked

was warning, don't go courting danger now, just don't,
and Tikas took a Cretan's offered cigarette,
and paced outside, and heard reports of soldiers close
to camp as if to infiltrate them in a time of joy,
wreaking some havoc he could only guess at. Louis
ground the butt beneath a polished Cretan boot,
found that he was staring at his own right hand
as if he were afraid that he did not exist.

What had he come to? He was twenty-eight years old
with a little money saved, no prospects for a wife
and family, his life a journey to a desert.
His hand, his own right hand had begun to tremble.
Too much responsibility had fallen hard on him
only because he did not shirk it, only because
he happened to work hard when people needed him.
Go find Tikas. Louis the Greek. He'll make it happen.

But he had been confused and often quite afraid,
without the good behavior of a martyred king.
He was no Christ. He knew it. He was ordinary,
small compared to men like Lawson. He was Tikas,
and who was Tikas? As the Scholar used to say
in Denver, "Tikas, you're a work of fiction—you're
so American you do not even know your name."
The Scholar. He could talk, but someone had to act.

—m—

Now comes the hardest day of all to write about,
clouded by myth and gunsmoke—April 20th,
1914, with Greeks still celebrating Christ
alive in the blue dome of Heaven, children playing
at the baseball field, Tikas paying a formal visit
at the Jolly family tent where Pearl invited him
for coffee and to look at picture postcards, awkward
in a momentary public show of friendship.

A neighbor woman joined them there and would report
they sat like friends and not like lovers until word
arrived that four militiamen had asked for Tikas.
He went out. Sunlight and dry grass. The slightest breeze
and, on it, smell of last night's beer, the cooking fires
banked low, coffee and light activity, and at
the camp's edge stood a corporal with three men
who said the strikers held a man against his will.

"What man?" said Louis. "No one tell me of a man."
They gave a name. Tikas said he'd never heard it,
which was the truth, but held his trembling hands behind
his back. "All right," the corporal said. "But we'll be back."
Louis turned to face the sunlight on the tents,
wearing this day his American suit and laced puttees,
seeing a group of women with *La huerfana*,
telling them no, there was no trouble—"All okay."

The girl he knew he'd seen at George Reed's mercantile
and it seemed odd to find her standing in the camp
with Mrs. MacIntosh, the Robles woman and
the others, talking of laundry or the baseball game.
He passed Pearl Jolly's tent and tried to catch her eye
as if to say, "Something's up," and went on to
his old tent where he had returned some days before,
and there he took a call from Major Pat Hamrock,

newly posted to the military camp, who said,
"Now Mr. Tikas, I understand your people hold
a man in there against his will, and I have spoken
to his wife who'd like to have him back. I understand
he won't be listed on your books and you can't know
every little thing that happens there, but you and I
have worked together well so far, and it would help
if you could find this man and have him brought to me."

"I do not know this man," said Tikas.

                                        "Well, then you
had better come yourself and talk the whole thing over,
understood?"

                "No, I do not understand."

                                        "You'll be safe."
"I'm not to believe you," Louis said. "I am not sure
you don't make a trap for me."

                                "If you don't come over,"
Major Hamrock said, "I'll have some soldiers bring you,
comprendes?"

                "No, I no *comprendo*. There is no man."
"Tikas, I have spoken to his wife. I order you."

And Louis hung up, pacing in his tent, alone.
Perhaps now Hamrock would be calling Linderfelt
at Cedar Hill to say the Greek was causing trouble,
bring down Company B.
Louis worried—had his voice betrayed his case of nerves?
He wiped his sweaty palms and called the Major back.
"Meet me at the depot, out in the open where all eyes
can witness—comprehend?"

Then "*Eláte paidiá.*" Outside his tent he gathered
Greeks he trusted, telling them that he would meet
the Major very soon and there could come some trouble
"but you must not cause more harm. Something today is wrong,
something I do not follow, but remember please
it does no good for us to go out shooting guns,
so keep the peace. Be patient. Wait until I'm back.
If you see Linderfelt, you know the danger's come."

He walked, weak-kneed, beyond the crossroads water tank,
the closed saloon of Ludlow to his left, the tracks
and depot right, and there he found the mustached Major
with a woman who seemed ill and very ill at ease.
"I don't know you," Louis said. "You have a husband?
Him I don't know either. Maybe he's a cripple
I saw Saturday night? We got no use for cripples
so we kick them out."

"Now Tikas," Major Hamrock said, "this lady said
you've got her husband. I've no cause to doubt her word.
Look over yonder." He pointed south where Louis saw
activity of soldiers at Water Tank Hill,
some sort of breastwork going up, machine guns placed
where they would have an unimpeded field of fire
north to the strikers' tents. "You see that we are ready
to cover an inspecting force if we move in."

Louis wiped his palms and thought of what to say,
but just before he said it from across the road
a woman called, "Will there be trouble?" Major Hamrock
turned stony, and that was when a young Lieutenant
dashed up to their meeting waving both his arms:
"Major, my God. Look at all those armed men up there."
They saw at once, a string of rednecks making for
the railway cut just east of Ludlow. They had shotguns.

"Please, I stop them," Louis said.
                              "Boy, you had better,"
answered Hamrock. And Louis ran as he had never
run before, muttering "God damn fools, God damn fools"
and reaching for the very kerchief he had danced with,
white, so he could wave it, "No!" And then: "God damn fools."
He heard his own steps on the gravel, almost to
the water tank. A bomb went off. He turned around
to see and as he ran a second bomb went off.

Then from the Berwind and Delagua roads and from
the breastworks back on Water Tank Hill, militia men
commenced their fire, or maybe strikers fired first?
The bombs were signals to the troops, and someone saw
armed strikers heading out of camp and set them off,
or so it seemed, but Louis could not understand
what brought the battle on, only that he had to save
the families in camp. Already panic ruled

as mothers dashed among the tents, snatching children,
fleeing bullets. Chaos of running people, screams
of men to lead the fight away from huddled tents.
Armed strikers fired from rail beds, fired from railroad cars
and bridges, aiming at the military camps
and south where two machine guns sputtered back at them.
Louis saw the skirmish at the depot, Hamrock
taking cover, and what looked like a soldier hit.

He saw the stronger women in the camp at work
to organize the others, leading them in groups
to safety in the wide arroyo to the north.
He saw Pearl Jolly, who touched his hand and met his eyes
and disappeared around a tent to do some work,
and then he fetched the rifle he had never fired,
a scope and belt of ammunition, starting for
the railway cut—but then he thought of Lawson,

turned back to his riddled tent and hauled the phone
to cover in the Jolly tent, set back a ways
and less exposed, where other men were huddled, thinking
what to do. He threw himself behind the cookstove,
scraping his knuckles on the platform boards, and rang
for Trinidad. Someone there got word to Lawson
who was coming. Next thing Louis knew, Pearl Jolly
crawled into the tent, a shoe heel shot off, and men said

the red crosses on her uniform made targets.
She started making sandwiches for the fighting men
and ducked when her bureau mirror flew to smithereens,
struck by bullets, and when the glass had settled, Pearl
went back to work. No time to talk. No time to touch
or look. Louis took two men and left her working.
Now the shooting was sporadic—men picked targets
when they saw them, firing carefully.

At the wide arroyo Louis found a line of rednecks
using the bank for cover. Many refugees
had made their way to safety, fleeing west beneath
the earthen lip to Bayes Ranch and beyond, but many
were flattened in the camp. Some hunkered in the pits,
some hid in the well or behind the pumping station.
He checked his watch and saw that it was not quite noon
as men arrived from Trinidad, John Lawson with them.

They had driven up, but left the car on prairie, east,
when bullets flew about them, then they made their way
to the arroyo. "I don't know why it start," said Louis.
"They call me in like we're gonna bargain, then I see
they're setting up to kill us." He was shaken now
and shaking and John Lawson took hold of his elbow.
"Not your fault, Louis. They picked the fight. I'll return
with help from town. For now, you keep your people safe."

"My friend," said Louis. "You always been good to me,
even in bad times." He could feel how close to tears
he was and pushed them deep within.
                                    "Just stay alive."
The two men hugged, his face as high as Lawson's chest.
"Make sure you tell them, Lawson. Don't let them forget
you got a lotta brave people out in the camp.
I gotta get back to help them now." And Louis crawled
over the earthen lip, then ran into the tents.

—⁓—

Pearl Jolly, who had taken food to fighting men,
found Tikas and declared she needed bandages.
Whenever she got close to the dispensary
some yahoo opened fire on her. The two of them
lay huddled, chaste, behind a mound of stolen coal
while bullets sent up spurts of dirt and flying gravel.
They were still there when a man crawled near them, his face
tear-streaked, and said his oldest boy had been shot dead.

Bill Snyder was the man. His boy Frank had been hit
in the head by a machine gun, nothing they could do
but stay pinned down in the deep pit beneath their tent,
but now he sobbed, "What do I do? My boy is dead.
He was eleven, for God's sake. He just stood up
and it hit him like that and he went down so fast
I didn't see it happen." Dirt started flying
and Snyder ran for cover while the Greek and Pearl

dashed from tent to tent, shouting to those in the pits
to get to safety in the arroyo when they could.
Running, they saw dogs and chickens shot, a wounded
fellow crawling as best he could.
The shooting came in waves now, steady as the sea
but heavy, light and heavy once again from all
directions, separate skirmishes around the camp,
then in the camp, where troops and rednecks dodged each other.

Linderfelt had brought a car right into the camp,
his troopers following, and while he raided tents
for anything worth taking, men brought gasoline,
and sometime in the evening tents were set on fire.
The southern end of camp was burning. Men ran in
to fight the fire; machine gun bullets drove them back.
Pearl and Louis sent some fifty people north
to the arroyo, rescued ahead of racing flames,

but there were clearly others in the pits. Their screams
were audible—or were the screams the flames themselves?
The bullets screaming in air? Louis tried to move
back in to the southern camp but shooting stopped him
so he found his cover, watching troopers move among
the flames, upending hatches, hauling women out
and herding them aside with sobbing children, looting
anything they could before they spread the flames.

At first he leaned against the pumping station wall,
his legs sprawled out before him, holding both his hands
above his useless rifle as if to claw the air.
The weight of his exhaustion seemed to press him down
and Louis Tikas saw that everything was lost,
the battle lost, the strike, the cause, that he had failed
John Lawson, Pearl, *La huerfana*, the whole damned camp.
Brute force had won. Brute force controlled the heavens now.

The light almost the light of Greece without a sea,
as if a million years had passed since early morning
and he was older now, much more than twenty-eight,
and this was Crete without salt water, the warrior dance
of villagers. Slabs of piney desert, thorns
and stones and sacrifice and endless killing rage.
He'd never crossed the ocean. This was a bad dream.
No—a bullet fell nearby, and it was real.

Darkness was coming on and rednecks had pulled back,
and Louis, too, joined Pearl and other refugees
in the arroyo. The smell of smoke was everywhere,
pot shots and licking flames where people's livelihoods
had been. "Catastrophe," he said aloud. The men
beside him had few cartridges, and where was Lawson?
He told them to retreat, east to the Black Hills,
and set his rifle down. He would go out, he said,

unarmed, and try to bargain with the enemy.

—⚏—

Canvas burns and wooden platforms burn, and Bibles
burn, and furniture, beds and dressers burn, and clothes
and picture postcards burn, and gnarled walking sticks burn,
hats burn, old protest signs, sheet music, violins,
guitars burn, boots burn, and money burns, though troopers
liberated money where they found it, taking
chairs and glass lamps, anything that looked worth keeping
for themselves, and Louis saw this looting and kept on walking.

He had been exhausted. He had worked all that day
to save the camp and failed, and now he kept on walking
till boys in uniform whooped he was their prisoner
and walked with him at gunpoint in the oily smoke,
taunting him: "We got you. A murderer. Know
what happens to murderers? We gonna string you up."
This was absurd, of course, but he said nothing. Yes,
there were dead—the Snyder boy and maybe soldiers,

but none of this was murder, none of this was his,
and still the camp was burning and there might have been
more people hiding in the pits. He had to find
an officer, someone with responsibility.
Now some thirty or forty men surrounded him,
searched him for weapons. These were men of Company B,
and Linderfelt strode among them, who would later say
he had seen Tikas silhouetted against the flames.

Gunshots from the east—perhaps retreating rednecks—
to no effect here at the crossroads water tank.
and Louis saw the red of flames reflected on
the faces of the men he faced, and saw dark hills
to the west, hills he had never yet grown to love,
a dry forbidding land. And then Karl Linderfelt
came up close with his rifle, shouting in his face,
"I thought you were gonna stop this thing, you little runt."

"Please," said Tikas. "We need to fight the fire. Please help."
    "Your boys are shooting at us. God damn it, we got dead
and wounded here and you said you were gonna stop it."
    And Louis couldn't help himself. He said the word
he always said to Linderfelt to get his goat:
"Someday."
            He saw the rifle lifted, raised his arms
to shield his face. The wooden stock came down across
his arm. Both broke—the wood and Louis's guarding arm.

And Linderfelt roared out like an animal, wordless
in rage, and looked as much surprised by the broken stock
as Louis was in shock at his dead arm, the way
it hung there, numb and longer than an arm should be.
His head was bleeding too, and now he was afraid.
He stood there with his useless arm as it began
to throb and send up shooting pains. He was not alone—
Jim Fyler stood there, also taken prisoner,

and with him a man called Bartolotti. Linderfelt
turned all three over to one Sergeant Cullen, walked
off with his cracked rifle, cursing. Louis saw him
move out of the light and wished that he had met
instead with Major Hamrock, a man who might control
his anger.
                    Now Linderfelt was gone.
                                        The soldiers shoved
their prisoners and Louis staggered half a step.
He looked at Fyler, who could only shake his head,

and maybe someone said, "You boys better run"
or maybe the broken arm, the line about lynching,
spooked them, but at once Jim Fyler ran, and Louis after,
ran for the Black Hills where distant rifles sputtered
out beyond the flames. And then a shove like someone
slapped him on the back and he was down and slapped,
slapped hard, and that was gravel in his mouth, and he
could not quite move his arms . . .

14. *The Death Pit*

Luisa waited with her huddled friends
all night by the Bayes Ranch where the arroyo
took them. The rifle fire was aimed away
toward the burning tents and down at Ludlow.
At last the nurse, Pearl Jolly, met them there
with refugees from camp, her hair disordered,
and said she feared not everyone escaped.
It was strange when peace descended with the night,

the stars above them startlingly clear
except when smoke obscured them. All that day
Luisa wanted to run back like Pearl
and help among the tents,
but Mrs. and Señora held her back,
not knowing where their husbands were and saying
she was young and she could not understand
the danger here, she did not know these men.

It was the sort of thing George Reed would say:
You're young. You cannot understand. This world
is dangerous. You will not live forever.
But they couldn't know, these older people,
how much she felt her life
was hers to hurl into the flames forever,
how often she had wished to die. Instead
she huddled, numb, against the sheltering rocks.

Word came a man named Costa had been shot,
a man named Frank Rubino, the Snyder boy. . . .
Rednecks had moved east of the camp it seemed,
the battle lost, the flames still shooting up
as if to scorch the stars, then headlamps shone
from cars and trucks, more shooting to the south,
and in the dark where mothers counted children
everyone was waiting for the night to end.

—⚬⚬⚬—

On April 21st the Ludlow camp
lay smoldering, its ordinary life
all burned away, except for bedsprings, wire
and woodstoves, some of them caved into pits.
The land was raked now by binoculars,
and several viewers would report that day
spotting a woman walking like a ghost,
a cinder among the ruins, stumbling, stunned.

And then another woman at the pit
below tent 58 was tearing at
the ground and shrieking, and some demented fellow
thought it a good idea to shoot at her.
Two women, Mary Petrucci, Alcarita
Pedragon, blackened and in total shock,
having crawled out of the smoldering pit,
went dodging bullets toward the depot, south.

The camp now like a junkyard of steel hulks,
stove pipes and burned stoves, the battle
stalled as if worn out,
and by the railroad tracks three bodies lay—
Louis Tikas was known by his brown puttees,
and when the news came up the arroyo, Pearl
sat down among consoling women, weeping,
Luisa watching things beyond her knowledge.

—◊—

Lawson had tried to make it back on foot
with reinforcements, but the heat of battle
kept him off. On the new day he set out
to organize the orderly withdrawal
of all survivors back to Trinidad.
Sometime that day the men of both sides learned
twelve bodies had been found in one of the pits.
They suffocated under the burning tent.

By this time no one had control of rednecks
fighting from New Mexico to Pueblo
with guns and bombs, anything they could steal.
Employees of the company were killed,
scabs were burned alive in shacks, and chaos
swept the plains and canyons everywhere.
Eighteen dead among the strikers,
and by the railroad tracks at Ludlow camp

the bodies of Louis Tikas and the others
lay untouched for three days,
horrifying passing passengers
on trains, who stared out windows at the maze
of wreckage that had been a union camp.
Newspapers sent their best to Trinidad
to find the Death Pit mothers. By a dim lamp
Mary Petrucci said she wished she'd died

with her smothered children. She still hacked smoke.
When interviewed, one trooper cracked a joke—
"We gave them Greeks an Easter they won't forget"—
at which he laughed and bummed a cigarette.
And much of this Luisa overheard
in shelters, helping worn-out friends to feed
those too much in grief to eat. Then George Reed
came with Sarah to find the girl. "A word,"

he said, taking her aside from the crowd.
But he could not begin to say aloud
what he had planned to say. Instead: "We've brought
some blankets from the store. Is this your cot?"
"The idiot," said Mrs. Reed. "Of course
he never says a thing right when he must.
Our children pine for you, and Pud is just
beside himself. He's liable to get worse."

"Young lady," said Mr. Reed. "We have come
to ask you to consider coming home."
Luisa looked at Mr. and Mrs. Reed,
at refugees around her, still dead-eyed
with shock, and many of their men had gone
to fight as long as fighting still went on,
and she was nearly weeping. She would lose
some part of her no matter what she chose.

Part Three

Interlude: January 16, 2003

> Writers drown for a living,
> teachers talk for their bread.
> I'm talking under water
> in this lonely motel bed.

And so the silly song goes dancing on in my mind. Last night I wrote, threw pages on the floor and re-wrote, wanting the lines to carry the story, not impede it. Wanting clarity. Wanting to drown without impediments.

Then I read the oral histories, the collage of voices in Papanikolas's book, and woke in the motel wondering if I could ever pull together my own version.

What are we to do? We, the ungrounded ones? How can we ever complete the story?

I drank the motel coffee, ate the motel toast, decided not to call my cousins in Trinidad because it is hard to have a conversation when you're drowning. Never mind the drought, the dust, the Purgatory River like a muddy wash.

198 ∽ Ludlow

On the east side of town the Catholic cemetery. On the west the
Knights of Pythias—the Masons, as I know them. I drove across the
river, up Goddard Avenue, then in through brick pillars. At the office I
asked for the grave of Louis Tikas, and the keeper got up from his
computer, straightened his pony-tail with both hands as he thought, and
gave me simple directions. He didn't ask me why I sought that grave.

What a change. When Papanikolas wrote his book the grave was
unmarked, its wooden plank rotted long before, so neither he nor the
aged Mike Livoda could find it. Now I found a large, pink granite slab
with U.M.W. symbol and these words:

LOUIS TIKAS
BORN: ILIAS ANASTASIOS SPANTIDAKIS
LOUTRA, RETHYMNON, CRETE, MARCH 13, 1886
DIED APR. 20, 1914, VICTIM OF THE LUDLOW MASSACRE
ORGANIZER FOR THE U.M.W.A.
PATRIOT

I wondered if he would wince at that last word, then thought, *No, he
fought hard to earn it.* Just north of the mesa known as Simpson's Rest,
with an unimpeded view of Fisher's Peak, an archetypal flat-topped
mesa, Tikas lies among other immigrants, Polish, Japanese, Hungarian,
Italian—all Americans.

My grandparents, Abraham and Ethel Mason, lie about 75 yards to the
north and east. Abe died in 1970, Ethel in 1982, and I stood in that
graveyard thinking, *Christ, twenty years I've been coming here and I never
knew who Tikas was or where they buried him. Twenty God damn years.*

The feeling of drowning again, of knowing all the currents of the story surround you though you cannot hold them. You're losing the thread of your story even as you tell it. Abe was maybe 17 when they shot Tikas. He must have seen the funeral procession winding down Commercial Street, across the river and up the hill—a mile long say all reports. This after the bodies were photographed and put on display—martyrs for the movement.

And three years later Abe joined a Scots-Canadian regiment, the Seaforth Highlanders, was shipped overseas and got himself wounded at Amiens in the summer of 1918. I visited the regimental headquarters at Fort George near Inverness, and the kind old man who kept the records found his name in their big books and photocopied the pages for me. There it is. Wounded. Amiens. 1918.

And there's a stone for Abe. A stone for Ethel who could talk all night if you let her. A stone for Louis Tikas, dead at twenty-eight just like my brother, Doug, was dead at twenty-eight. But no stone for Luisa Mole, none for the Reeds, so many others. Where did they go? I write for them as well. And I write, as they say, for myself. I write of them to feel more alive in my own skin, as if my existence were finally as real as theirs.

I took the long drive west on Highway 12, past Cokedale and the numbered towns—Primero, Segundo, Tercio—following *El Rio de las Animas Perdidas en Purgatorio,* past Stonewall Gap, through Cuchara Pass, then downhill to La Veta, on into Walsenburg, which seems so sleepy now. On the way home I would take the freeway exit and the gravel road out to *El huerfano,* a moonscape in these days of drought, and stand there for a long while with the orphan, as if it might whisper its stony secret in my ear.

15. *Stonewall Gap*

Windblown aridity in early spring,
piñon, prickly pear, the struggling scrub.
At noon my shadow pooled beneath my boots,
my eyes surveying ground a step ahead
for arrowheads or any signs of life,
out walking a friend's ranch with Abraham,
the land a maze of dry arroyos, slabs
of pale rock, the flints exposed by weather.

There too the terrible remains of winter,
dead cattle caught in a raging blizzard
lay unthawed in postures of resignation.
I was so intent on treasure that I stumbled
into a ditch and fell across the corpse
of a calf the wild coyotes dined upon,
a gutted leathery thing—it had a face
and I started backwards, stifling a scream.

What was I? Twelve years old? The age I dreamed
Luisa Mole out foraging for water. . . .
On our visits south
I begged to be taken to the mesa country
as if those afternoons on skeletal land
put me in touch with some essential code,
the remnants of a people who moved through,
migrating hunters five millennia past.

Look for a bench, land flat enough to camp on,
a nearby source of water—there you'd find
the silicates in flakes, clear fracture marks
where fletchers made their tools, the midden washed
by wind and flash floods all across the scarp.
Nothing remained in place here. Even trees
had shallow roots. In dustbowl days my father
picked up points by the dozen on this land,

pot-hunting like his neighbors, half in love
with science, more with the electric touch
of hands across receded seas of time.
What had we found? I knew this evidence
of other lives had meaning of some sort.
I saw the strangers, grew among them for years
in my own mind. But was it love or envy?
Was it only pride of place? A kind of theft?

Always looking at the ground beneath my boots,
always listening for the call of Abraham
who'd find a point and let me think I found it,
whose meaty, sun-burnt hands would leave the pool
of wide-brimmed shade, point beyond scarred boots
to the perfect knife, worked like a stone leaf
and left there by the ancient wanderers,
original, aboriginal, and magic.

—⁓—

Eventually one has to list the names,
these the people smothered in the Death Pit:
Cedelina Costa (whose husband died
of gunshot wounds elsewhere in the battle),
Lucy Costa
Onafrio Costa
Cloriva Pedragon
Rogerlo Pedragon

Frank Petrucci
Joe Petrucci
Lucy Petrucci
Patria Valdez
Elvira Valdez
Mary Valdez
Rudy Valdez
Then others shot, including Frank Snyder:

Carlo Costa
Frank Rubino
James Fyler
John Bartolotti
Louis Tikas
And, of course, the wounded, and one dead trooper,
Private Martin, mutilated in the fight,
some said, by a redneck with a gnarled hand.

All crossed the gap, whatever gap it is,
between the presence and the other side
that is, perhaps, no other side at all
but another form of presence, absent
to us as at times our own existence is.
All walked the earth, or as small children crawled,
and wondered at its panoply—and this life
goes pushing through, much like the winding road

aimed west from Trinidad through Stonewall Gap,
a space between the fin-like, mineral outcrops
where the river has a purpose of its own
flowing the other way, east from the mountains
down through Trinidad, among dry mesas,
grasslands, then out to the Arkansas,
on east to the Mississippi and to the Gulf
and—who knows?—maybe all the way to Crete.

News of so much death flew up the Front Range
like migrating birds in high Armadas, north,
much of it distorted for propaganda.
The Greek was dead, his funeral was grand
because the union needed something grand.
May God pardon all his sins.
May his memory be eternal.
And may the earth rest over him lightly.

That last bit said traditionally in Greece,
but the eyes of heaven are no living eyes,
some people still insist, compassionate
or fierce. They are the blankness over all,
beautiful and empty as deep space,
the diamond-hard reflections of the stars.
And nothing is the word of peace,
nothing will offer love. . . .

—∾—

No word of peace in the mines of Aguilar
and none in Walsenburg, none on the roads
or in canyons. Bombs and hostages and fire.
A bankrupt state that could not pay its Guard
now turned, suppliant, to the President
in Washington, and Federal troops were sent.
And all this time upstairs in his Broadway office,
Rockefeller Junior watched the tape

that bore the news that made his passive face
contort, a sort of wrinkled countenance
he would smooth out when he put on his coat
and bowler hat to step out to his car.
There was construction of a family home
to see to, there were children to be raised,
and after all, he had his competent men
to answer accusations in the press.

He would not see descriptions of the bodies,
though later, facing a committee, he
would face a picture of the Snyder boy
laid out as if asleep on a plank, but not,
because it was not visible, the back
of the boy's skull blown entirely away.
He would not read the wounds of Louis Tikas—
one bullet from the back through the right lung

exiting his chest, one as he spun came through
the right hip and struck a vertebra, then
pierced the stomach and the diaphragm.
A third came also through the hip. Noted
as well, the injured arm, the wounded scalp.
It was determined Tikas bled to death,
unlike Jim Fyler, whose face was blown off
by a bullet that had entered from the rear.

No, these details would not disturb the office—
only, months after the strike's defeat
his secretary came to tell him women
waited outside his office. They had been brought
by Mrs. Upton Sinclair, and of course they were
the Ludlow women on their national tour.
They would report a sad-faced gentleman
came out to look at them, and then the cops

arrived, escorting them outside the building.

—∞—

That tour would surely have been a sight to witness,
the incoherent Mary Petrucci who
had lost her children in the pit, Mary Thomas,
the singing angel Luisa had met in jail,
and as a special heroine, Pearl Jolly.
The union paid expenses, put them up
in good hotels. Long articles appeared.
In Washington they met the President.

But the cause was lost. That summer World War I
erupted overseas. Few Americans
were in a mood of generosity
and fates closed in like thunderheads on others:
Karl Linderfelt would face a murder charge
with Sergeant Cullen. Neither went to jail
and Linderfelt became a sort of drifter,
drunk and bitterly denouncing enemies.

Strangest of all would be the murder charge
against John Lawson, isolated now
by union higher ups.
He beat the rap but found himself at forty-
something hefting a pick into the dark
and hacking a crude existence from the seams.
He ended up in management, his talents known
and well rewarded. Miners always said,

"If Lawson makes the contract, we will sign it."

—ɯ—

Most who had joined the strike could get no work
and wandered like the scattered tribes to cities
all across America. Cash Jackson
got his job back as a guard and later worked
in Pueblo with his old friend, MacIntosh,
but Lefty Calabrini, good with guns
and dynamite despite his crippled hand,
could find no work except the random jobs

for businessmen in Trinidad, hauling,
house-painting, cutting grass, whatever came
his way and paid for food and cigarettes.
One day he found himself, weary from walking
in search of work, at rest upon a stone
beside the river, when
a girl who seemed adrift, her long hair
tied back, her body in a shapeless smock,

came up to him and saw that he had trouble
rolling a cigarette with one good hand.
Without a word she took the makings up
and smiled at him and licked the paper, then
rolled another for herself. "God damn it,"
Lefty said, cupping a match for both,
"I see you around. I see you and think
that girl looks exactly like her mother."

Beside them the river flows from Stonewall Gap,
the limbs of cottonwoods fan in the breeze
over the muddy waters. Looking up,
they stare at sunlight flashing through the trees,
and then across at buildings, loading docks,
the heavy traffic on Commercial Street.
They smoke together. Neither of them talks.
She kisses him, then makes a slow retreat.

16. *A Stone for Luisa Mole*

One of those brick buildings by the river
used to have my family name across it.
There Abraham had manufactured candy,
a struggling concern my Uncle Frank
took over at Abe's death. When we were kids
my brothers and I eyed the sugar vats
on Colorado visits, scooped our hands
in barrels of sweet stuff.

In college years I took the Trailways bus
to Trinidad and stayed with Uncle Frank,
Aunt Marge and all my cousins at the house
off Victoria Square. Some days I went to work
with him, meaning we had to rise in the dark
and drive across to the loading dock where Frank
unlocked the office. Then we strolled around
to Commercial Street and in the back door

to the kitchen of the old Savoy Hotel,
a Chinese cook cat-napping by his grill,
and into the café, where businessmen
would gather for thin coffee, cigarettes
and all the latest jokes.
No one could tell a story like my uncle,
who loved to tease the girls and play a hand
to see which friend would have to get the tab.

I think of all those faces in the old
Savoy, a hotel then long past its prime
with letters bleaching from its café windows:
the fire chief, a guy who did construction,
men who owned shops, men who played in bands,
their faces stained and wrinkled by the sun,
their laughter hearty even in hard times
when dry weeds seemed to overcome the town.

And in the corner booth a little woman,
part Mexican, with salt and pepper hair
and dark eyes clouded by some memory. . . .
I put her there, I know, out of desire
to see that she survived
at least into the 1970s.
She wears a sort of shawl, a woven cloth
with Indian designs. Her hands surround

a coffee cup. Thin, bony fingers,
chapped perhaps from washing dishes, face
still beautiful but wan and sunken.
A life of care? The sunspots say a life
outdoors, perhaps a life of wandering
or a life of penetrating sunlight.
The eyes betray a life with some mistakes,
a haunted life, undaunted yet subdued.

The men are laughing at another joke
about the salesman and the farmer's daughter,
comfortable men at home in Trinidad
who've known each other since their grade school days,
who went to war together, then came home
to raise their sons and daughters in the town.
But I keep staring at the corner booth,
the lonely figure no one else can see.

—∞—

Finding Lefty by the river made
Luisa almost sorrowful at leaving,
and though he was more than twice her age she wanted
to stay and kiss him more, as if she might
assuage his suffering by giving love.
And she was lonely living at the Reeds'
with work to do at home and at the store,
and books that she could take into her room.

Books had always meant a vaster world
of kings and sufferers, far seas and ships,
lands where everything green shoved into life
and would not stop its elbowing for space.
A world she never felt was hers to live in
without some work of tending other souls,
as if she lived on only at the grace
of people who were born knowing their place.

In 1915 little Pud was five
insisting everyone should call him George,
so Little George he was. And Casey Reed
at ten had taken up piano—badly
but persistently at least. Her sister Marty
at eleven wanted horses in the meadow
while Libby, twelve, was always chasing boys,
and Daisy Reed, thirteen, loved scholarship.

The oldest girls had had their periods
and Daisy spent three days a month in pieces
having to be consoled by older women.
Luisa, too, had always been hit hard
by cramps and bleeding, but had to tough it out
and concentrate on chores. Nowadays it seemed
with every tub of laundry there was blood
from somewhere in the house

and Mrs. Reed insisted Little George
not see this evidence of changing bodies.
And there was more Luisa Mole could not
disclose—the night when Arthur opened her door
(George had gone to bed) and filled her room
with smoke-and-whiskey smells and said to her
to make no noise and made her use her mouth
to bring him off. She had more stains to wash,

hiding the evidence so well that Arthur
came and came again into her room
and moved her off the squealing bed and mauled
and bit her nipples, stumbling back one night
when he had tried to force her and instead
discovered he was holding bloody gauze,
and stared at it uncomprehendingly,
then gave it back and left her sobbing there.

So she met Lefty by the river, smoked
and let him touch her as they kissed, and he
the constant fighter, knew by a strange instinct
at least the gentleness that she desired,
surprising in a thick-set man who'd lived
for decades by ferocity alone.
He kept his gnarled hand at her back and moved
his good hand underneath her flowered smock.

And one night in the spring, with a full moon
that made the lawns and trees of Trinidad
look bluish underneath the shadowed mesas,
Luisa stuffed her clothes in a gunnysack
and left the sleeping house and ran downhill,
her spirits lifted by a warm chinook
that seemed to flow above the flowing water,
and found him pacing by the river bank.

That night the lovers dodged the railyard bulls
and hopped a freight before it rolled from the yard,
sharing a car with yeggs and hobos bound
wherever it might take them. By first light
the countryside that passed outside the slats
was dry and open. It was New Mexico,
her mother-country, land she'd never seen
except in stories that her parents told.

This much she could do. She could give and give
and make of giving something of a home,
her body trembling, ready to receive
and fill with the desires of others—all
she knew for certain she was good at ever.
And he, though he could never say sweet words,
led her beyond the Purgatory Valley,
making a kind of safety in the world.

Their fellow travelers took her for the daughter
of the scarred man beside her. They were careful
not to act like lovers in the boxcar
though its swaying often pressed him to her body.
Lefty hadn't shaved, and his close-cropped hair
stood on end, and she wanted just to touch it,
wanted to console him for his battles,
wanted to offer him a life of peace.

—∞—

When Arthur Reed received the news about
the runaway, the blood drained from his face
but he said nothing. In the shop with George
he did his work, and after work he went
alone into the White Front Bar and drank
six shots of whiskey in a row, deciding
that no, he'd not be over to the Reeds
tonight for supper.

For years the younger George would think about
Luisa, how inconsolable he'd been
at five when she ran off. He was convinced
that immigrants had come, like coal mine ghosts,
to spirit her away and steal some food
from his mother's larder. There was no ransom note,
no note at all, and as a young man George
would sometimes dream the body of Luisa,

the way her arms had wrapped about his shoulders
and his head fell back between her breasts and he
could smell the smell they said was Mexican.
It wrecked him, really, almost as it had
his uncle Arthur, who turned into a drunk
and died in 1934. Young George
worked in his father's store, and then they moved—
the lot of them—to Denver where his sisters

made good marriages, the family prospered
and little George was called Big George because
he stood a full head taller than his father.
The Reeds grew with the city, building homes
in towns that would become the suburbs, even
learning how to ski. George Reed Junior owned
new cars, trading them in after the second year,
fathered three children by his rodeo queen,

and after burying his long-lived parents
and bossing two sisters through their divorces
and seeing his sons go into medicine
and law, and after Rotary and golf,
his own wife's struggles with the bottle, after
business cycles that he thought would break his heart,
and "two-bit governors" who were Democrat,
George Reed died in 1995.

The papers said he'd led a happy life.

—∽—

Luisa can't have been so lucky—her start
in life was harder. Lefty Calabrini
couldn't ever settle for one woman.
Perhaps in Italy no one would blink
to see an aging man with a child bride,
but they were never married. Even here—
amnesiac America—they had
a checkered prospect. Lefty looked for work

in Arizona copper mines, and there
fell in with gamblers who would make him rich,
or so he thought. This was in the mountains
outside Tucson where Luisa swept
the floors and made beds in a big hotel.
They had a small room in a boarding house,
no questions asked, and for some weeks were happy,
Lefty slamming their bed against the wall

until he came, Luisa holding on
as if she gripped a bronco's underbelly,
wondering if this was love. One night he lost
at cards and tried to kill a man, and Lefty
took a bullet in his forehead. Waiting
well into the night for his return,
before the lawman pounded on her door,
Luisa knew for certain he was dead.

She stayed awake and thought of Lefty, knowing
nothing would bring a dead man back to life,
but holding a picture of him anyway—
a man who could be kind, a man who laughed
until he shook with coughing, squeezing tears
from squinting eyes, pulling her close to him
and rubbing her hair. But there were bad days too
he came home fairly burning with his rage.

He had a pauper's grave, just like her parents.
Luisa promised she would buy a stone one day
but never did. She met a woman named
Adelle and they rode freights
clear out to California. Somewhere in
Los Angeles I lose all track of her.
The land is large, the century recedes,
names change, perhaps with marriage or divorce.

Why is it that I see her back in Trinidad,
a town you hardly notice passing through
above the rooftops on the Interstate?
What could have taken her to Prospect Street
and other painful scenes unless she wanted
to go ghosting back, searching for some peace?
I see her walking, looking through the graveyards
for familiar names and finding none. She is

a woman in her sixties now, alone
with yet another life, another man
behind her, maybe children that she writes to
back in California. She has come here
to visit scenes of childhood that might tell her
who she is. The years have not been easy,
not on her, not on America,
with fresh assassinations and more war.

And little wounded Trinidad persists
among the buttes, the scrubby piñon trees.
The muddy Purgatoire persists. Just north
of town outsiders, Hippies, build a commune
called Drop City. Geodesic domes
made of the sun-bleached hoods of salvaged cars
rise from wooden platforms like the Ludlow tents,
and for a while they take Luisa in,

sharing their food and dope, and in exchange
she watches their children, gives them advice
on how to live outside the status quo,
but she can see the commune will not last;
no dream of freedom does.
People always fall into old patterns.
One night, though, they build a giant bonfire
outside in the open desert, and that night

Luisa tells them stories of the mines
and how this land was full of immigrants
who fought and lost, and most have moved away.
The communards, disciples of a man
who came here from the east, are young, long-haired
and not attuned to history. They smile,
smooth-skinned, open-faced, holding children
tight on laps in the flickering light of flames.

Suddenly she sees them with fresh compassion—
they give and give without a single thought
of payment. It isn't history they want
but present life, each instant a new session
cut off from the past, alive until spent,
young desert swimmers trying to stay uncaught
by ordinary nets. Though they will fail
she cannot think them foolish in their trial.

Talking, she turns a small stone in her hands—
a trace of ashes rubs off on her skin.
At the edge of light a tall jackrabbit stands,
apparently transfixed (its body thin),
but is it by her voice or by the fire?
The fire whiplashes sparks into the sky.
They seem to live as stars, or else to die
into the breezy midnight, desert air.

What can she give but her own stories, told
to willing ears? She turns the tiny stone
once for her mother, then for poor John Mole,
for Lefty, Too Tall and the others gone
beneath hardscrabble surfaces with love.
And everything they were in vanished graves
except for the passing moment that she saves,
the dome of heaven blue, dark blue above.

I dream Luisa gathering her story,
no trace of her parents' accents left in her,
though they are part of her life's inventory.
She uses names like Tikas, Rockefeller,
Lawson, Mother Jones. The communards
have heard of some of these, and she unveils
a vision of the camps in simple words,
a scrap of song, a memory of hills.

Map

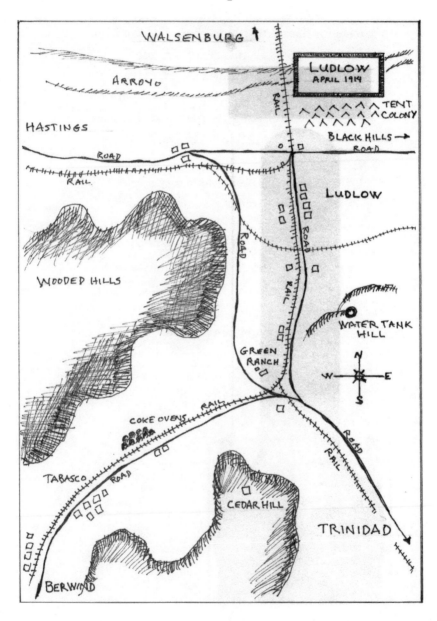

Afterword

Fiction, Fact, and Verse

> "For one reads what one likes—yet one writes
> not what one would like to write, but what one is
> able to write."
> —Jorge Luis Borges

The story of *Ludlow* has lived in my marrow for forty years, and I tell it now because it feels ripe and I feel ready. I knew it was a story long before I told it, long before I even did research on the historical facts. I knew it when, as a boy, I first laid eyes on the dry mesas north of Trinidad, Colorado. I have made my experience and that of my family part of the story, which freed me to change focus at will, move about my imagined landscape with greater flexibility than I had attempted in earlier narratives. What excited me about this story was not any political agenda, but the elements that have always obsessed me—family, landscape, immigration, language. It was already part of my life's work before I had written a line or found myself inventing a girl named Luisa Mole.

As in another narrative poem of mine, *The Country I Remember* (1996), this work braids fact and fiction the way an historical novel would do. There is far more fiction than fact, and "facts are not the story," as I say in the text. When *The Country I Remember* was first published, one critic assumed that I had just set down family stories in verse, as if he could not imagine a poet actually inventing characters as well as scene-building details. Most of that work is fiction, not only in the sense of being made up, but also in the techniques employed. The same is true of *Ludlow*, though of course several characters and events are based upon fact. Friends have asked me to set the record straight—what is history, what fiction?— and I will do so briefly here.

The one major character based upon historical fact is of course Louis Tikas, or Ilias Spantidakis, and I have made no secret of my debt to Zeese Papanikolas's book, *Buried Unsung*. That book gave me a great many details and was itself inspiring in its prose style and interrogative method. The arc of Louis's story as I have given it here owes much to Papanikolas and other writers, though I have also felt free to imagine Louis's mind, using my own experience of having lived in Greece. I even gave him a sex life. Though there really was a Pearl Jolly and though rumors abounded about her and Tikas, we don't in fact know they were lovers. We do know that Pearl was uncommonly brave during the events at Ludlow, and we know the gist of how Louis died that night. For readers who would seek more of his life, I cannot recommend Papanikolas's book highly enough; it is a brilliant and deeply moving investigation.

John Lawson was real—and a real hero, as far as I am concerned. His betrayal by the U. M. W. is one of the union's more disgraceful chapters. My scenes with Lawson are largely invented or "reimagined" from sketchy facts. Likewise Karl Linderfelt, who was if anything more a racist son of a bitch than I have painted here. Pat Hamrock was real, as was Governor

Ammons, as was Ethelbert Stewart. General John Chase, accused of corruption, was forced to resign from the militia in 1916 and died two years later. Frank Snyder and the other Ludlow victims are all given their real names in my account. Those names appear on the monument at Ludlow, which gives Tikas's age incorrectly as 30. The monument was vandalized in the spring of 2003—apparently what it stands for still gets under some people's skin. Jeff "King" Farr was forced out of office not long after the massacre, and has passed into legend—a corrupt sheriff suitable for Hollywood. And of course Mother Jones was real. Even her lies were real. Her highly colorful autobiography is worth reading. She really was held under guard at a Trinidad hospital. There really was a women's march in protest where General Chase ordered a ridiculous charge and fell off his horse.

Many of these events did take place as I have recounted them. The Death Special really existed and really opened fire on miners more than once. The Baldwin Felts detectives were at least as brutal as I have made them here. The shootings in and around Trinidad and Walsenburg really took place. My job, though, was to make events comprehensible to the minds of my characters, to give them some "ground sense." I wanted to use the drive, economy and rhythms of verse to make a compelling version of a story I could not get out of my system. The fact that I have spent much of my life in southern Colorado, where my family goes back four or five generations, certainly did not hurt. Nor did it hurt that many of my family members loved to tell stories. The voices of my grandfather Abraham and his four sons still sound in my head. They are among the most powerful influences on my writing life—as powerful as any book. It was my Uncle Tom who first gave me *The Great Coalfield War* by George McGovern and Leonard Guttridge. And my Uncle Frank was a veritable fount of detail, much of which, alas, had to be pruned away for the sake of narrative compression.

A minor character in my book, because I wanted to focus most on ordinary people where I could give imagination free reign, John D. Rockefeller, Jr. was of course a major player in all these events, though he seems to have been ignorant of the hardships of his employees. He reminds me of other people who live life by a theory more than by experience. His laudable idea that people ought to be free and independent of collective bargaining could only have been held by a man ignorant of the violence and injustice of people's actual lives. I've heard of others who wanted life to conform to a theory, and Rockefeller was certainly not the worst of them. They're usually just wrong, rather than wrong and dangerous. Rockefeller's ignorance was dangerous to a lot of people, but to give him credit, he had already established philanthropic credentials with the Rockefeller Foundation in 1913, well before the massacre. In 1915 he toured the southern coal fields with his friend, the Canadian politician Mackenzie King, who had more experience with labor relations and helped Rockefeller establish better communications between labor and management. King was also a more openly gregarious man, and at a gathering in the town of Sopris he got Rockefeller dancing with the miners' wives, which proved to be good public relations. Many years later, Rockefeller acknowledged having learned much about humanity from King, who had gone on to become Prime Minister of Canada.

One doesn't want all the historical context in a work of fiction, of course—just enough to give the story some legs to stand on and to acknowledge the truth, such as it is. Most other characters in *Ludlow* are invented: Luisa Mole, her parents, the MacIntosh family, the Reeds, Cash, Lefty, the women of the camp, the Scholar and Dimitris. I'll admit to using family photographs to help me picture the Reeds, but they are otherwise quite unlike my great-grandfather, George Mason, and his tribe.

—⁓—

Anyone who writes narrative verse will confront a version of the following question: *Why didn't you just write it in prose?* The assumption underlying this question is that prose is the proper medium for storytelling. After all, no one really takes verse seriously any more except for the poets, adherents of a counterculture of one sort or another. Prose is thought to be more lucid and true to the tale—easier to read, closer to how people really understand life, etc.

This, I would argue, is an impoverished view.

It's not just that I have literary history on my side and can cite vital narratives in verse from Homer to Frost. It's not just the perpetual popularity of new translations of ancient works, or that my own generation has seen a resurgence of interest in narrative and dramatic verse, from figures like Anthony Hecht and Louis Simpson to Vikram Seth, Andrew Hudgins, Mark Jarman, Chase Twichell, B. H. Fairchild, Dana Gioia, Marilyn Nelson, Rita Dove, Robert McDowell, Sydney Lea, Brad Leithauser—a woefully incomplete list, to be sure, though it does include some of our ablest contemporary poets. The fact that narrative verse continues to be written does not entirely justify it as an art form, or so many literary editors might claim. Narrative verse may well be popular when performed, but few are eager to publish it. For one thing, it takes more space than lyric poetry. It's like a rapacious tree that crowds out smaller plants.

There have been champions of narrative verse, including the poets listed above and the editors of a few journals such as *The Hudson Review, The Paris Review,* and *The New England Review.* These angels are just like anyone brave enough to publish imaginative writing these days, whether prose or verse. We live now in a culture of nonfiction and the even more popular media of film and music. A few good novels can break through to a popular audience now and then; a few mass market periodicals still publish fiction, and one can't help relishing the fact that Seamus Heaney's vigorous version of *Beowulf* was a bestseller. But I would still admit that writing stories in any form is a risky business, and writing them in verse is positively quixotic.

Nevertheless, I do not see why this must be so. To begin with, verse is often more cinematic than prose in its rhythms and images, its narrative economy. When I worked in the movie business in the 1980s I met a film editor who was also a poet. Over drinks in a Beverly Hills bar, we discussed similarities inherent in the two media, the poem and the movie, and I came away feeling that one was more popular than the other only because it was usually more passive. Reading takes more effort. Nowadays, teaching difficult poems by, say, Eliot, I often begin by asking students to make an imaginary film in their heads as they hear the poem performed; it's remarkable how much understanding can take place before one gets down to the usual business of analysis. Poems can speak rather more directly than they are sometimes given credit for.

Narrative verse is not inherently harder to read than narrative prose. In the right hands, verse actually has more clarity, drive and economy than prose, and it can offer literary pleasures of a sort unavailable in other genres. Take a look at the old Scottish border ballads—poems like "The Wife of Usher's Well" and "Sir Patrick Spens"—and you will see how a simple stanza allows the poet to eject reams of exposition. Speakers of dialogue don't need to be identified but are inferred from context. And that same quatrain stanza can be used for lyric repetition, a rhythmic underscoring of tones and themes. One can see these techniques at work in a more recent poem such as Elizabeth Bishop's "The Burglar of Babylon," as good a ballad as any I know.

Look at the short narratives of Robert Frost—poems like "Home Burial," "Out, Out—" and "The Witch of Coös" and you will see how blank verse technique can be used to dramatic effect. A line break can illuminate psychology, put an extra twist in dramatic tension, impressing tonal shifts more subtly than sentences alone. There is a culture of verse that is different from the culture of prose, but just as capable of engaging great subjects at length.

Of course "Home Burial" is a mere 115 lines long, though every bit as intense as the best Pinter play. What happens to that intensity when you move to book-length narratives? The truth is that it falters on occasion, just as prose novels have their peaks and valleys. Rising and falling language, like rising and falling action, is part of the experience of the longer work. Poe famously objected to the long poem on these very grounds, suggesting that the quotient of poetry would be diminished the longer the poet kept going. He had a point. Homer apparently nodded. Even Milton gets a bit much now and then, doesn't he? I would be lying if I insisted that lyric intensity could be sustained indefinitely, though these old masters performed remarkable feats.

But lyric intensity is not the only component of a narrative poem. There is also the story, and if you have a good one it will have a form of its own. To me, the story is a remarkable and irreducible element of humanity. Stories are forms every bit as much as sonnets and ghazals are, yet even the most traditional stories allow for the subversive imagination of strangers—readers—each of whom might experience the tale in remarkably different ways. Stories are stable in one sense, unstable in another, just as great lyrics may be coldly logical in form yet passionate in expression.

In his Harvard lecture called "The Telling of the Tale," Jorge Luis Borges concluded,

> . . . there is something about a tale, a story, that will be always going on. I do not believe men will ever tire of telling or hearing stories. And if along with the pleasure of being told a story we get the additional pleasure of the dignity of verse, then something great will have happened. Maybe I am an old-fashioned man from the nineteenth century, but I have optimism, I have hope; and as the future holds many things— as the future, perhaps, holds all things—I think the epic will come back to us. I believe that the poet shall once again be a maker. I mean, he will tell a story and he will also sing it. And we will not think of those two things as different, even as we do not think they are different in Homer or in Virgil.

It is my fervent hope that Borges was right, that we are ready again for stories in verse.

—David Mason

Biographical Note

David Mason's previous books of poetry include *The Buried Houses*, *The Country I Remember* and *Arrivals*. His book of essays, *The Poetry of Life and the Life of Poetry*, appeared in 2000, and he has also co-edited several anthologies and textbooks. A former Fulbright Fellow to Greece, he has published work in such periodicals as *Harper's*, *The Times Literary Supplement*, *The Nation*, *The New Republic*, *Poetry* and *The Hudson Review*. He teaches at The Colorado College and lives in the mountains outside Colorado Springs.